Western Lands and Waters Series

IX

THE UPPER NARROWS AT VICTORVILLE
From a sketch by Inez Page Huffman

THE MOJAVE RIVER
AND ITS VALLEY

*an ancient river, and the story of
its discovery, its paradoxical nature,
its service as a pathway for migration,
and the progress of its valley*

by

ERMA PEIRSON

THE ARTHUR H. CLARK COMPANY
Glendale, California   1970

TO

VIRGINIA MACDONALD

Whose love for her fellowmen
added richness to the story of
THE MOJAVE RIVER AND ITS VALLEY

Contents

Illustrations

Foreword

In 1956 a desert book of considerable importance saw publication. Its name — *Kern's Desert*; its author — Erma Peirson. The first edition, twice reprinted, went quickly out of print. The book supplies a comprehensive historical coverage on a score of towns and areas in the Kern segment of the Mojave Desert.

In my bibliographical study — *Desert Voices* (1958) — I included this assessment of *Kern's Desert*:

> Desert lovers have long awaited this book. Our Bibliography laments the paucity of literature relating to the great Mojave Desert. With the exception of Death Valley, and of the Old Spanish Trail route stretching from Cajon Pass to Nevada, little or nothing of descriptive value has been written of this vast desert area — save Marcia Wynn's excellent *Desert Bonanza* and occasional magazine releases. *Kern's Desert* supplies a recognized need, and supplies it well.

In 1966 Russ Leadabrand authored his *A Guide to the Mojave Desert of California*, perhaps our most important literary contribution to the Mojave, in the sense that it covers almost this entire desert area. The three volume set of *Mohahve* (1963-66), produced by the Victor Valley College and the Mohahve Historical Society, assembles valuable illustrative and descriptive material on the Mojave River country.

Now, in *The Mojave River and Its Valley*, Erma Peirson significantly extends the scope of her *Kern's Desert* coverage. Using the age-old river as her central theme, she weaves around it a brilliantly researched tapestry of historical lore. There are chapters relating to the early day visitors, the first ranches and towns, the remote canyons and valleys, the courageous settlers who pioneered this lonely land that sprawls along its ancient river.

And a most remarkable river it is, this ninety-mile length of the desert river. Remarkable — and consistently unpredictable. Rising in the towering San Bernardinos it flows north and eventually northeast, both *over* and *under* the desert sand, alternately disappearing and re-appearing; emerging, in season, to flow deep and wide and swift between abrupt canyon walls; finally to lose itself forever in the desert sands. For mile after mile, portions of the river channel may remain substantially dry for a period of several months, with little or no surface water showing; but an underground movement is all the while forcing the hidden flow downstream. Only where subterranean rock formations push the stream upward from the porous alluvium does the water appear on the surface. This built-in characteristic of the river to escape beneath its sandy bed enables it to retain much of its water load that would otherwise dissipate itself in rapid surface evaporation.

To Francisco Garcés goes the honor of being the first white man of record to discover this unusual river. On March 9, 1776, he noted in his *Diary*: "I found a stream-bed with rather brackish water and named it the Arroyo de los Mártires."

Jedediah Smith crossed it in 1826, and christened it most appropriately — "The Inconstant River."

Fremont saw it, described it, named it. In April of 1844 he wrote: "A clear, bold stream, 60 feet wide, and several feet deep, had a strange appearance, running between perfectly naked banks of sand. . . As we followed along its course, the river, instead of growing constantly larger, gradually dwindled away. . . After riding 20 miles in a northeasterly direction, we . . . halted. The trail followed still along the river, which, in the course of the morning, entirely disappeared. We continued along the dry bed, in which, after an interval of about 16 miles, the water reappeared in some low places. . . A short distance below, this river entirely disappeared. . . I heard it called by the Spaniards the *Rio de las Animas*, but on the map we have called it the *Mohahve river*."

Historically, the Mojave River was ever a welcome landmark to the vast number of emigrants who followed the Old Spanish Trail across the treacherous Mojave Desert. To them it meant water, pasture, rest. Even more importantly, it signaled the near-end of their strenuous desert trek. Some fifty or sixty miles beyond was the Cajon Pass — their gateway to destiny. Typical of the reaction of these early travelers upon their arrival at the river are the words of the Mormon James S. Brown, a member of the San Bernardino contingent of the Jefferson Hunt wagon train in the early winter of 1849. Writes Brown: "When we reached that stream, I presume we felt as pleased as a man liberated from life sentence in a dungeon, for we had reason to feel assured that we would succeed in our journey, . . . (with) plenty of feed and water for our stock, with time to rest in. Some shouted: 'Daylight once more; thank God for our deliverance!'"

Erma Peirson's love for the desert and its river reflects itself pleasantly in her new book. She *knows* the Mojave; is sensitive to its every mood and caprice. It is her homeland. She has researched its early history and has identified herself with its subsequent development. Moreover, she is equipped — both by educational attainment and by personal contact — to write intelligently of it. As a result, her book radiates warmth and companionable understanding for the river and desert she knows and loves.

"Strange river of the Mojave!" she writes. "Born in springs and icy streamlets, nourished by brooks that take the waters as their own, and by creeks that pour into the two mainstreams of the mountains, which — by their confluence — become the Mojave River that takes up the burden to find existence in a land needy of its wealth. We had found peace up there near the sky, and had stored within ourselves a beauty to share with the future. We had climbed a mountain and had seen glory — the glory of a beautiful land that should one day be known for its fairness because of these waters we had looked upon. We tucked the day's wonder and joy in our hearts to take out in the delight of memories."

Author, newspaper editor, and dedicated student of California history, Erma Peirson qualifies as one of our foremost interpreters of the Mojave Desert. *The Mojave Desert and Its Valley* qualifies as one of this desert's distinguished books.

E. I. Edwards

Yucca Valley, California

Preface

Eminently qualified to write a history of the Mojave River, Erma Peirson has accomplished a task that has been recognized by California historians as one requiring not only a profound knowledge of the region affected by this strange stream but an awareness of its significance in the history of the West.

Erma Peirson's writings on desert subjects have long been regarded as authoritative. Hundreds of articles have come from her prolific scholarship, and her book *Kern's Desert* has attained a high rank in the literature of the West.

It has been my privilege to be aware of her knowledge of the Mojave Desert and her skill with words for more than a score of years. To me, her work is worthy of the honors that have accumulated in her behalf and I am personally convinced that the history of the Mojave River will in time be recognized as the standard work on the subject, a classic that will rank with the best of its kind in the literature of California history.

This book has been years in the making; her researches have been long, exhaustive and thorough. The presentation will commend itself to scholars and lay readers without exception. It will indeed fill a need that has long been felt by students of California history.

RALPH F. KREISER

Kern County Museum

Acknowledgments

A river is the cosiest of friends.
You must love it and live with it
before you can know it.

George William Curtis,
from *Lotus Eating*

Long before this volume became a reality it had been worked out in thought processes for some kind of presentation to the world. A great deal of information had been garnered and something had to be done about preserving it. To those who have been aware of this project through the years, and have encouraged and aided me to bring it to fruition, I am most grateful.

To my family I say "thank you" for your patience and understanding of a dedicated plan of work.

A very special feeling of gratitude is extended to Mr. E. I. Edwards for his critical reading and helpful suggestions on the manuscript, and for his excellent "Foreword." Further thanks are due also to Mr. Edwards for his descriptive bibliography, *Desert Voices*, which was published in 1958. The thorough coverage in that volume obviates the necessity of a bibliographical section in this book, except for certain specific footnote references.

For help in research I am indebted to the following libraries: Naval Weapons Center Library, China Lake, California; Fresno County Library and its branches at North Fresno and Gillis; and San Bernardino County

Library and its branches in Apple Valley and Victorville.

I am indebted to L. Burr Belden for the use of over twenty years of his historical articles in the San Bernardino *Sun-Telegram*; to Caryl Krouser who opened his thirty-year files of news records in the Barstow *Printer-Review*; to R. V. Morrow for lending pictures and historical papers; and to the Right Reverend Monseigneur James H. Culleton for the use of his personal copy of the Garcés diary.

For the use of pictures that add to the unfolding of the Mojave River story, I am very grateful to all those who are identified in the illustration captions.

Special appreciaton is extended to Martin J. Snow for preparing the map for this volume; to Inez Page Huffman for her rendering of the Upper Narrows which appears on the dust jacket and frontispiece; to Theresa Jackson Butler for typing the final draft; and to Ralph Kreiser for the "Preface." I am grateful for the desert books and magazine articles of Dr. Edmund C. Jaeger; and to Dr. William C. Leone for his artistic sketches from old photographs.

To all who have patiently waited for the publishing of "The Mojave River and Its Valley," I am grateful that you have been interested.

ERMA PEIRSON

September, 1969

PART I

Sources and Beginnings
of the Mojave River

To Needles

π_5

Snow '69

River Paradox

It is with rivers as it is with people—
the greatest are not always the most
agreeable nor the best to live with.

Henry Van Dyke,
from *Little Rivers*

Where is the Mojave River?

One might well ask that question when starting out over California's Mojave Desert to locate its elusive river — that inconstant river of sudden appearance and even more sudden vanishing.

But there is a Mojave River, incredulous as it may seem to one unfamiliar with the eccentricities of the desert. And the Mojave River can boast of an ancient heritage. Its actual age goes back milleniums; and its known recorded existence measures barely short of two centuries. Perhaps this river would have been easier to locate millions of years ago when it was reckoned in the upper echelon of rivers, for surely its geologic history substantiates the theory that it was a river of mighty force. This ancient river was powerful enough to carve a channel through the stoutest of rock even though it could easily have swerved around a barrier and cut a new chasm in alluvium.

Macadam and concrete roads now lead across the Mojave Desert following the Mojave River bed. The only evidence of a river might be the line of trees beyond a highway where a sandfilled channel curves through the desert expanse.

How do you know there is water out there on the desert as you speed along in your modern car? The reason is obvious. You can see the vegetation at almost any time of the year even in the piled masses of sand dunes. Although it may be difficult for one unfamiliar with the desert terrain to detect the usual signs of a river, yet the signs are there if you can read them — river sand, trees, lush grasses, green alfalfa fields, and the hum of pumping plants; all these indicate a possible river somewhere near.

In due time you will know there is a river out there in its sandy, living bed. You will be certain to learn of that freakish river, the Mojave, which has earned such an array of descriptive names as it has meandered along through the years — names such as Upside-Down River, Hidden River, Inconstant River, River of Mystery, and River of Martyrs. You are going to learn it is a wrong-way river and a runaway river.

First and last you will discover the river to be one of contradictions; that it rises in a lovely pine-ridged mountain country in a high and lofty range where ice-cold springs run out of rocky crevices; then turns its back on its fine beginnings and flows down the wrong side of the mountains and into the lowlands of a languishing desert. You will note, in time, that at its end it loses all contact with the world and disappears into utter nothingness.

You will find that this strange and paradoxical river flows underground through granite basins, boring its way through alluvium and pervious rock; then where it reaches impervious rock, it comes to the surface and flows on top of its channel of sand and alluvial materials. If, when you start your search, it is a season of heavy rains and much melting snow in the mountains, you may be able to see the river rolling along as any self-respecting river should.

At Barstow, outpost of the desert, there is a constant sign of the river down in the lowlands near the railway tracks and sand shows damp in many places under the bridge over which countless people travel daily, perhaps most of them unconscious of the historic river bed below. You will find, too, that at Barstow the river has often spread out a mile wide in times of flood.

You are going to find that river. When you do, it may appear as only a strip of sand; yet it is never empty of water. For there, sheltered from the world above, snug in its chambered course, it flows along through sand. And if you question the use of the word "flow," perhaps a more appropriate word would be "seep."

You may be so unaccustomed to desert regions that you will intensely hate the Mojave and lament the fate that brought you to such a desolate land. Mostly you will hate the river that, so far as you can see, is not a river at all. You can't swim in it. You can't fish in it (under normal conditions) and you can't sail a boat upon its waters. And where are the river breezes one naturally expects to enjoy when living in a spot by a river? What good is a river like the Mojave anyway? Where are the ports? the wharves? the pleasure vessels? the industries? Surely a river has some of these advantages. Certainly there is no millstream type of living out here on this great expanse of desert vegetation and on the endless sands of times.

You don't like the sand. You can't tolerate the dry old desert. You don't like the barren hills, nor the wide, lonely spaces. The rocks look so uninviting, all hot and tumbled. The wind is so exasperating as it blows curtains of yellow sand across the valleys.

Where is the beauty? Where is that all-absorbing, all-powerful, irrestistible charm of the desert that gets such a grip on people? Every person who comes to the desert must discover that for himself or herself.

The beauty? It is found in the contoured hills and the folded mountains with shadows and lights; in the variety of the colors, shapes and sizes of the rocks; and in the sharp wind-chiseled dunes. It is there in the desert-blue skies; in the flaming hues of the sunsets when the master paint-box seems to have been upset and all the colors have blended into nameless shades. It will be found in the ethereal quality of the desert dawn and in the soft, white mists along the river on a winter morning. There is never a desert dawn or sunset repeated. In fact, when consciously watching either to note the changes, it is impossible to see the hues and patterns take form when the sky reveals new images. The transformation happens so suddenly, so intricately, so softly and quickly that the human eye cannot discern the split-infinitesimal point of time in which the changes are made.

The Mojave River has no tributaries along its desert course. It is a lonely, lazy river; a silent stream that is an instrument for water distribution over much of the Mojave Desert region — equal in size to the combined areas of New Jersey, Massachusetts, Rhode Island, and Connecticut.

There are many people who have explored the river from beginning to end. From the time when the Mojave Desert was settled by homesteaders and others, and towns were established, the interest in the great American Desertland grew. Federal surveys have been made and recorded. Universities and colleges have added the study of the desert regions of the Southwest to their curricula and the world is becoming more knowledgeable of this great American Desert.

The old Indian trail across the desert was a difficult one, but of all the trails leading into California it was one of the easiest and safest.

None of the emigrants, not excluding the Spanish priest who was the first known white man to see and follow the Mojave River, left one word of the beauties of the desert. The sunsets, the color-splashing sunrises, the great spring wild-flower sweeps, the wide expanses that take on special beauty when rimmed by snow-clad mountains — all these were the same two centuries ago as they are today. But desert travel in those early days was beset by perils of the unknown. The travelers were hungry and thirsty. They lost most of their stock to starvation and the Indians. Many became ill. Some died by the wayside. Under such stress and strain, emigrating could have been no pleasure.

Through the far-flung expanses of the Mojave Desert, the Mojave River winds and wends its way through unusual terrain of rock and sand, of grasses and shrubs, and a few native trees. Its history, make-up, and propensities are such that it has become one of the most extraordinary waterways known — perhaps its duplicate can be found in no other part of the North American continent.

In the days of the pathfinders and explorers, the old Indian foot-trail (widened by use) was called Old Indian Trail, Garcés Trail, Mormon Trail, Mojave Trail, Salt Lake Trail, Government Road, and Old Spanish Trail. The Old Spanish Trail, which was a continuation of the older Santa Fe Trail, was the most lasting of the names. The Salt Lake Trail and Government Road merged at Yermo.

The old trail was used by many nameless Indians who lived along its route, or traveled it to the Pacific Coast from the inner regions of the Southwest. Such journeys were made to obtain seashells which the inland Indians prized highly.

The trail was also traveled by zealous padres who came from Old Spain and Old Mexico to serve their king in the new country as they attempted to carry their religion to the savages of the new land.

It was a highway for trailblazers and pathfinders — those dauntless men who paved the way for civilization of the West. There were gold-seekers and the hardy miners who passed along the desert trails, and many remained to make their own rushes — gold, silver, borax.

Land-hungry people sought virgin territory in the West for homesteading, and they rolled over the desert and along the Mojave River in large numbers. Civil War veterans came to make a new start in life and many left their imprint on the region as they searched for home sites and fertile soil.

The source of the Mojave River was an important

medium in the westward march of civilization. It offered its channel and shorelines for the restless travelers of several eras. It provided life-giving campsites for rest and succor. Today there are few places along the Mojave River where water is visible at most times. In the middle 1940s, the river flowed above ground at nine places; that should have been just as true a century ago when the teeming emigrants crossed the desert. Less water was taken from the river for farming and domestic use during the great western migration than is done today. In these later years a great amount of water is pumped from the river for irrigation purposes. Also, there have been many dry seasons through the years which have contributed to the lowering of the water level of Mojave's basins.

The manner in which the waters of the Mojave survive the thirstiness of the desert sun is one of the strange features of the odd Mojave. The rate of evaporation is extremely high in the desert. Did the river not conceal its waters within its sands, they would not last long, for the sun is a powerful enemy of the Mojave River.

The old trail became a highway of crime. Renegade white men and marauding Indians preyed on the ranchers and stockmen, stealing and driving away their stock. They also made raids upon the passing pioneers, massacring them and appropriating their animals. This finally brought about the establishment of forts, manned by soldiers for protection of the people.

The paradoxical desert river proved one tangent of America's manifest destiny.

THE OLD ARMY BRIDGE ON THE MOJAVE'S WEST FORK
This picturesque bridge, of World War II vintage, spanned the
stream less than a mile above its confluence with Deep Creek. A
wooden bridge had served here many years until it washed away
in the flood of 1938, after which the river was crossed by fording.
This bridge, soon to be demolished, was used until 1968 when
the Arrowhead road was realigned.
Photo courtesy of Myra McGinnis.

2

Strange Waterway

Rivers are highways that move on,
and bear us whither we wish to go.

Blaise Pascal, from *Pensées*

Rivers have traditions which may have been built upon legends or actual events that brought settlements to their banks. In the founding days of the West, pioneers sought localities near rivers. A river means many things: water, crops, stock, power, travel, communication, transportation, and homes.

When the descendants of the early American colonists trekked westward, it was along the courses of rivers that most of them camped and later built their homes. Trading posts were often established near river shores that would grow into settlements; then into towns; then to progress to cities.

Rivers have made history for countries and communities. They are seldom quiescent. They have challenged — perhaps as a small stream urging itself to the sea, or as a mighty force carving canyons in great stone barriers. A river is an impelling force — so it cannot stand still. It defies people to cross its waters, to conquer its compulsions, to build industries, to carry on its trends of civilization.

In America's past many rivers have beckoned the passers-by with rich drainage valleys; with lush banks of plant life; with pools where animals could drink; with thickets to protect birds; and with wild fruit, nuts and fertile soil.

The Mojave River did not have such a heritage to offer the pioneers that crossed the desert. Its chief offering was its means of being a pathway. It was a courageous thing for the emigrants to attempt crossing what appeared to them as desolate land — for it was harsh, unrelenting, and treacherous. But they came in spite of the tales of horror they had heard even before leaving their homes — wind, pounding and fierce; sand, blinding and painful; with thirst unquenched; the sight of bleached bones of animals, burned wagons, and roadside graves. Much of it was true, much was imagined.

The Mojave River was there waiting, secreting in sandy depths its life-giving waters, which it doled out to the travelers who followed the desert trails. The Mojave is the only river that runs through the Mojave Desert. It finds its course in the headwaters of the San Bernardino Mountains. It *rises, flows,* and *ends* in land-locked San Bernardino County.

From some compulsion in the earth (that occurred eons ago), the Mojave's unnatural divide sends the waters of the mountain slope north and east. The headwaters sweep over two hundred and fifteen square miles of the area. The waters flow through marshes and meadows, past pungent pine trees, through gorges far back in the mountains, and from high levels, including the Lake Arrowhead region.

Many tributaries contribute to the two main streams — Deep Creek (often called the East Fork), and the West Fork of the Mojave. These streams are considered as "The Forks." At the point where they merge, the waters flow over rocky terrain. Here the Mojave proper dips under the sands of the ancient river bed and quite literally becomes an underground river. There where rivers blend their waters, the sand has been deposited for centuries upon centuries. This deposition of sand has caused the river to be built to a higher level, which is at variance with most rivers.

The Mojave's first unorthodox quality is due to faulting. The lower area of Deep Creek is approximately fifteen miles from the San Andreas Fault.[1]

The San Bernardino Mountains intercept the coastal rains, which fall in great amounts, increasing as they reach the crest. On the desert side of the mountains the precipitation diminishes. The timber growth is mostly of the smaller varieties of mountain vegetation. The roads become narrower, often hugging the mountainside with precipitous inclines pointing down the deep ravines.

Deep Creek receives tributaries from nearly two-thirds of the watershed; the West Fork gathers a little less than one-third. The basin of Deep Creek is from two to three thousand feet higher in elevation than the West Fork area.

Deep Creek rises in Holcomb Valley and flows through a trough-like gorge. It has always been a fisherman's paradise. The West Fork meanders through Summit Valley where a canyon road runs through the area, opening out on magnificent views of the rugged region. The West Fork flows through the old and famous Las Flores Ranch.

---

[1] Koebeg & Koebeg, Engineers and Architects for the Mojave Water Agency, *Supplemental Water Report,* 1962, p. 14.

The West Fork crosses the old Lake Arrowhead Road about seven miles from the town of Hesperia which is built on a mesa. Where the road crosses over the river, there is a high mountain which is part of the boundary line of the San Bernardino National Forest. The road makes a delightful bend on both sides of the river where cars waited their turn to cross because of the narrowness of the small iron bridge which has spanned the stream since World War II. This bridge, which is less than a mile above the confluence of the West Fork and Deep Creek, is an old Army bridge, called a Bailey Bridge. According to Jesse Peterson of Hesperia, regional road superintendent of West Desert Area Eleven, the significance of this type of bridge is the easy facility of installing or removing it with only about two or three hours time being involved. Mr. Peterson was head of an operating equipment crew of the county, and supervised the installation of the bridge. An old wooden bridge had spanned the river but it was washed away in the great flood of 1938, after which the stream was crossed by fording until the Bailey Bridge was installed.

The bridge is a pre-fabricated structure with steel sections. It received its name from D. C. Bailey, an English inventor who designed it. The bridge faces removal and is not in use now. Road realignment has changed many features here in the vicinity of the Mojave Forks Dam which is in the early stages of construction. The legal land description of the point of confluence is Section 18, Township 3 North, Range 3 West.

At Victorville, about fourteen miles from the union of the rivers, the waters of Mojave pass through a rocky canyon called Upper Narrows. The gorge is one thou-

WHERE RIVERS MEET — DEEP CREEK AND WEST FORK HERE FORM THE MOJAVE
following the spring rains of 1967; a popular retreat for swimming in past years.
This flow has been repeated annually, except in years of extreme drought.

Photo by Ruth Rutledge.

sand feet long; its granite walls are three hundred and sixty feet apart and rise to one hundred and fifty feet.

About three miles north of the Upper Narrows the river passes through a smaller canyon which is called Lower Narrows, near the town of Oro Grande. Surrounding geologic conditions are similar in both gorges. Bridges span the stream at both Narrows.

There is always water in the region of the Upper Narrows. The rocks at both the Upper and Lower Narrows act as barriers, back of which ground water is partly impounded and the result is that the water is brought to the surface and causes the river to become a perennial stream between the two Narrows.

The channel in the Narrows is filled with sand and gravel to a depth of about fifteen feet, where bedrock is struck.

The two Narrows present an interesting geologic feature. The river cut its present channel through hard rock when it could easily have followed what appears to be a simpler course by turning westward to make a channel through the soft alluvium. Geologists explain this uncommon adaptation by assuming that the present course of the river was determined at an earlier period when the river valley was filled with alluvium, covering the spurs of the mountains on the east where the Narrows are cut. As the river cut down the channel it encountered bedrock and gradually cut into the granite until the canyon was formed—thus the present drainage has been superimposed on the old rock hills.[2]

---

[2] David G. Thompson, "The Mojave Desert Region, California, a geographic, geologic, and hydrologic reconnaissance," in U.S. Geological Survey, *Water Supply Paper*, no. 578 (1929), p. 302.

The Upper Mojave Valley includes the Upper Mojave River lowlands, West Mesa, El Mirage, Fifteen-Mile Valley, Deadman Valley and Sidewinder Valley. The Middle Mojave Valley encompasses the area between Oro Grande and Barstow, including the Helendale region. At Barstow the Lower Mojave Valley begins and covers the territory to the terminus of the river's course.

The Mojave River not only brings down countless grains of sand through its channel from the mountain foothills and through the desert, it also carries in its wake great boulders and large rocks. At a flood control meeting in Barstow a few years ago, a film was shown of an actual Mojave mud-flow which brought down roiling muddy water along with stones and huge boulders.

As an aid in understanding the carrying power of running water, the following excerpt is taken from an article titled "Up-Side-Down River," by veteran desert writer Philip Johnston. The article appeared in *Touring Topics* in the November 1929 issue.[3]

> Through countless milleniums, the waters that find their way into this river have been at work, developing features that have few parallels on this continent. Incredibly slow, but incalculably potent, these elemental forces have wrought an outstanding example of the versatility of Nature's most useful tools—erosion and alluvial deposition. It is a well-known fact that the carrying capacity of running water varies directly as the sixth power of its velocity. In other words, when the speed is doubled, the carrying capacity is increased sixty-four fold! This explains why a stream, flowing at the

[3] *Touring Topics* has been succeeded by the title *Westways*, both published by the Automobile Club of Southern California.

rate of three miles an hour can move only small grains of
sand; while the torrents unleashed by a cloudburst and foam-
ing down a mountainside at twenty miles an hour can roll
boulders weighing tons.

Twenty miles from Yermo the flat desert changes to
very rugged terrain in the area lying between Cady Mountains and Cave Mountains. The high ground formed a
barrier between the two ranges, which it is believed,
dammed the waters of the Mojave River ages ago. A
weak section in the barrier gave way to the great eroding force and a gorge was cut. Cave Canyon (now
called Afton Canyon) was formed as a result of the
erosion and is a graphic illustration of this ancient
river's mighty power.

The present day Mojave River finally reaches this
canyon and carries its waters to an outlet. In the canyon
it flows on the surface of its bed, winding through a
meadowland of pastoral scenes. When the waters leave
the stream bed, they flow onto Crucero's sandy plain and
find channels that carry them to Soda Dry Lake. A portion of the outgoing waters go over into the Cronise
dry lakes.

The terminus of the Mojave River is called "Sink of
the Mojave" which is in line with the geologic nature
of this river and the fact that the river disappears rather
than flowing *into* any stream.

Beyond Soda Dry Lake is Silver Dry Lake. These
two dry lake beds are playas and hold surface waters
only in times of great floods. When Soda Lake is full
to capacity, surplus water runs through a natural trough
into Silver Lake.

In pre-historic times Death Valley (which is a playa

in the bottom of that great sunken land) was the last outlet for the ancient Mojave River. The playa in Death Valley is called Lake Manly. Death Valley was a pluvial lake as were Soda, Silver, and Manix Lakes.

The Mojave's length has been a debatable issue with many people. Flowing through hidden channels, and emptying into an undergroud basin rather than following the usual form of flowing to the sea, it is, at best, difficult and unpredictable of measurement. It is at the mercy of the elements. These elements of rains, snow, flood and sand sometimes cause the river to flow in extended or diminished channels, creating changes in its length. There may be many years between floods; again, the weather cycle may bring floods in several successive years. In any event, such occurrences can make changes in the physical stream bed.

Records show that during one period floods came in the years 1910, 1914, 1915 and 1916; the 1916 flood taking a heavy toll in the Barstow area. A county report stated:[4]

> The river had run rampant during the flood, taking out all the trees in the bottom land, scoured down at the south abutment of our 200-foot steel highway bridge, leaving this abutment tilted down, and the long steel bridge left in a distorted, torsional shape, though still standing. . .

Every flood leaves its wreckage of bridges and cut river banks, changing the stream bed. The history of the Mojave River runs rife with flood and damage, as well as lost lives. Flood control is coming to the fore in these later years, and time will prove the wisdom of its cost.

---

[4] San Bernardino County Flood Control District, *Dedication Bulletin*, May 1968.

In seeking to state a reasonably understandable length of the Mojave River, we turned to the Mojave Water Agency in Victorville. Mr. Carl Coleman, general manager of the agency, presented the following figures: Starting with the confluence of the two main streams of the headwater country of the San Bernardino mountain range, where these streams — Deep Creek and West Fork of the Mojave — have garnered the water above the Forks, the flow takes us across the desert plains for ninety miles to reach Afton Canyon, then flows through it to other outlets. The breakdown of the ninety-miles shows a northerly flow for thirty miles from the Forks to Helendale; a northeasterly twenty miles from Helendale to Barstow; and an easterly forty miles to Afton Canyon. Adding the canyon's four-mile gorge gives a total length of ninety-four miles.

From Afton Canyon the river comes to the Sink of the Mojave where the water disappears and wanders back and forth for fourteen miles, finding its channel to Soda Lake. The river then crosses the lake in a northerly direction for eleven miles. Here it goes through a two-mile trough into the six-mile length of Silver Lake. All told, we now find the Mojave's length to be one hundred and twenty-seven miles from the Forks to and including the length of Silver Lake.

There might also be added a few miles where, in flood years, the Mojave sends some of its waters through a gap into the Cronise Lakes. This creates what has been called the Little Mojave Sink.

When the length of the river is compared with the length of one hundred and forty-five miles mentioned by Dr. Edmund C. Jaeger in his book *The California*

Deserts, we find a difference of eighteen miles, which can be accounted for by the inclusion of the eighteen miles of the streams above the Forks. This would make the length of the river correspond closely with Dr. Jaeger's 145 miles. When discussing with Dr. Jaeger the length mentioned by him, he explained that when his first edition of *The California Deserts* was published in 1933, he did not himself measure the river, but took the figure from a descriptive railway guide book. That mileage has remained unchanged in the several editions of that book.

3

Mojave's Headwaters

Rivers need a spring . . .

George Herbert,
from *Jacula Prudentum*

Little and long, little and short, the mountain streams of the lofty San Bernardino sweep over slopes and across meadows, fed by springs that ooze out of hidden crevices. The streams that are formed murmur happily along, secure in the certainty they will find larger ones to add to the Mojave River when it is ready to take off with the headwaters they have been gathering, and flow north and east on the way to its career of oddity.

There are lakes in the mountain country. With few exceptions they are man-made. Lake Arrowhead, once a pastureland through which small streams ran, is an extravaganza of recreation today; it was once called Little Bear Valley. An irrigation dam was constructed on the site in early days.

A monument now marks the summit where the river's discoverer, Father Garcés, took the down-trail to the San Bernardino Valley after crossing the Mojave Desert in 1776. He had followed the Mojave River bed to its headwaters in the mountains.

When the Mormons settled on the Lugo Grant and established a colony in 1851 (now the city of San Bernardino) the men went into the timber in the mountains to cut lumber to build their homes. David Seely and his brother Wellington are said to have constructed the first sawmills in the high country, getting water to run them from creeks nearby.

Holcomb Valley was a colorful early settlement in the mountain country. William F. Holcomb, for whom the valley was named, came into historic fame for two reasons: as a bear hunter who seldom missed his mark, and as a discoverer of gold. He had come to the region in 1860 when there was excitement in silver and iron mining.

Holcomb started out one day for a hike — and a possible bear kill. Climbing to the ridge that separates the Santa Ana River and the Mojave River, he looked out over a beautiful valley. He explored the site for a brief time. Back at the camp, he told about the valley. It was immediately called "Holcomb's Valley." It bears the name to this day.

One day Bill (as Holcomb was called by his cronies) made another trip to his delightful valley, accompanied by a friend. When they reached the valley they saw a bear down in the center and each man took a shot at it. Neither shot killed the bear, but it was definitely wounded. They started after it but darkness came upon them before they caught up with it. The next morning they again took up the chase, following the bear's tracks until they came to a quartz ledge which they stopped to examine. The bear chase ended there and then — they had found gold. The bear was located later — dead and spoiled.

The camp at Big Bear had prospered and had grown into a busy settlement. However, Holcomb and several others decided to move over to Holcomb Valley and start a new diggin's. After settling in, Bill went hunting and brought down four bears with four shots.

As soon as the news spread about the gold in Holcomb's valley, many people rushed in. The gold was discovered in May and by the Fourth of July the place was swarming with prospectors and all the types of people that follow a mining camp.

On the Fourth a celebration was held and the miners raised a flag which was furnished by Mrs. Jed Van Dusen. In appreciation of her donation of the flag they named the camp Belleville for the Van Dusen's little girl, Belle.

Supplies were brought into camp by pack trains and the freight charges were exceedingly high. The miners decided to have a road built for wagon freighting as a means of lowering rates. They raised $1,500 by subscription and gave the job of roadbuilding to Jed Van Dusen, a blacksmith.

The wagon road led

> from Holcomb Valley westerly along the mountain range, passing by the Great Lead Mine, on by Coxey's Ranch, thence by Rock House, westerly down the mountain side by Rock Springs, westerly over a desert to the Mohave River, on southwesterly near where Hesperia is now, thence through the cedars to the head or summit of Cajon Pass, where the road was already made by . . . John Brown, Sr., leading to San Bernardino, and all Southern California. . .[1]

---

[1] William F. Holcomb, "Letter to the San Bernardino Society of Pioneers, January 27, 1900," in John Brown, Jr., and James Boyd, *History of San Bernardino and Riverside Counties* (3 vols.; Madison, Wisc., 1922), pp. 272-77. In this letter Holcomb reports the funds raised as being $1500; some other writers and students of the desert report the amount as $2000.

Later, roads were built in other directions from the camp. People continued to pour into the area. Merchandise was coming in at lowered prices. It is recorded that some $350,000 worth of gold was obtained by the primitive methods then employed.[2]

Both Bear Valley and Holcomb Valley were active in politics and mining. The influx of people brought with them a rough element, and shooting and killing were everyday affairs. The Belleville camp became a fiery center of secessionists. At one time Belleville had a population of two thousand. It was the largest voting township in the county in 1861.

Little valleys, short streams, high mountain peaks, old shady foot-trails, pine forests with pungent aroma, far vistas looking out over views akin to Bible lands, boundless reaches of daytime skies, comforting domes of night, the breath of light air — all combine to make the highland country as beautiful as it was when the first white man walked over it.

The Indians have gone. Wildlife has receded; it will not remain where there is excessive honking of horns and the confusion of traffic. Yet around the settled homes the small, pert squirrels become quite chummy, with gently offered portions of food.

Storms still come to the mountains with resulting rain and snow. The dogwood blooms in spring and summer. An annual "dogwood day" has been declared at Crestline where the trees are abundant.

A legendary history of the dogwood tree says that at the time of the Crucifixion of Christ, the dogwood trees

[2]George W. and Helen P. Beattie, *Heritage of the Valley: San Bernardino's First Century* (Pasadena, 1939; also reprinted Oakland, 1951), p. 366.

grew as large as the oaks and other trees of the forests of the Holy Land. The wood was firm, and it was chosen to use in building the Cross upon which Christ died. Jesus sensed the distress of the dogwood tree, that it had been compelled to serve in such a sad purpose.

Jesus promised never again would the dogwood tree be used for such aims; that henceforth it should be slender, twisted, and bent.

The blossoms, Christ promised, would be in the form of a cross with two short and two long petals at extreme ends; in the center of the outer edge of each white petal would be a nail print. (The dogwood blossoms run from four to seven petals.) The center of the flower would be brown, symbolic of blood stains. This legend is so old that its origin is unknown. It is unlawful to pick the blossoms in the San Bernardino Mountains.[3]

It is in this beautiful country that the waters of small streams gather to form the two main waterways, which, in turn, unite as one and flow out over the desert floor. Down in the desert flatlands there are no tributaries to check the wasting waters and they have gone unharnessed through the decades that the white man has used them. Year after year this has continued, and the story in geological times must have been similar, especially after the pluvial area.

The damming of a river is an important feature in a world of waters gone awry. From the time of the first settlers upon the Mojave Desert the problem has been of concern — what to do about the headwaters that become unruly when reaching the desert. Some of the unruliness starts with heavy mountain rains and melting snow.

---

[3] Earle Buie, columnist, San Bernardino *Sun-Telegram*, May 11, 1967.

As this book is coming into the stages of completion, man has reached a great milestone in the river story, and in a few years the happenings of centuries untold will be changed.

The Flood Control District of San Bernardino County has worked faithfully to bring about measures to save the waters along the river course. In May 1968, dedication ceremonies were held at the Forks site for the future Forks Dam.

Our Mojave River artist and the writer took off one day in the winter months for the Observation Point on the old historic Lake Arrowhead Road. It led into the skyline overlooking the two rivers as they merged into one channel. There is a splendid view of the foothill country and way beyond. As it happened, it was a glorious day. The winter rains had not started, the rivers were quiescent, and the old road was safe.

Seeing two rivers come together is a magnificent view. It was a wonderful sight as we drove up and up and looked down on the lower hills we had visited so many times. There, interrupting the placidity of the scene below, we saw the dam-building process at work. The site was changing under the hand of man and machinery. We had known the Forks in seasons of docility as well as in rampage. It is good to know the dam will bring productive value as the waters unite in storage instead of spilling haphazardly.

Strange river of the Mojave! Born in springs and icy streamlets, nourished by brooks that take the waters as their own, and by creeks that pour into the two mainstreams of the mountains, which — by their confluence — become the Mojave River that takes up the burden of

THE FORKS OF THE MOJAVE RIVER

This air view reveals the beautiful panorama stretching over the mountain sides. Here can be seen the confluence of Deep Creek and the West Fork of the Mojave River, as they carry their headwaters from the San Bernardino Range.

At this site the Mojave Forks Dam is being built.

finding existence in a land needy of its wealth. We had found peace up there near the sky, and had stored within ourselves a beauty to share with the future. We had climbed a mountain and had seen glory — the glory of a beautiful land that should one day be known for its fairness because of these waters we had looked upon. We tucked the day's wonder and joy in our hearts to take out in the delight of memories.

PART II

Discovery of the Mojave River

4

A Desert Priest

When you wander, as you often delight to do,
you wander indeed . . .

Francis Bacon,
from *Letter of Expostulation to Coke*

No white man, so far as known history is concerned, had ever set foot upon the shores of the Mojave River until the chance discoverer of the stream came through the Mojave Desert seeking a new route to the missions along the Pacific Coast. The desert was then uncharted, virgin territory. The discoverer was Father Francisco Hermenegildo Tomás Garcés, a dedicated missionary-priest who came to the new world at his own request. He proved to be the forerunner of many emigrants on the desert trail in that new world.

He was born in the Villa de Morata del Conde, in the Reyno de Aragón, on April 12, 1738. As the boy grew older his parents noticed that his mind had centered on sacred things, so they placed him under the tutelage of his uncle who was a curate in the birthplace of the boy. He was fifteen years of age when he sought holy orders. He completed his studies and was ordained for the priesthood when he was twenty-five. He went on to higher education, gaining a strong desire to be of use to others, and it was perhaps natural that he should choose to become a missionary.

The priest entered the New World of Spain at the age of thirty and was assigned to San Xavier del Bac, which was twenty leagues from the Presidio de Tubac, arriving there on June 30, 1768.

This was a part of the wildest area of Sonora. Garcés worked willingly among the Indians during epidemics and poverty. His life had been dedicated to self-forgetfulness; nothing daunted him. He was so dedicated to the work among the Indians that Father Pedro Font, diarist of the Anza expedition, painted a graphic word picture of Garcés:[1]

> Padre Garcés is so fit to get along with the Indians, and go about among them, that he seems just like an Indian himself. . . He shows in everything the coolness of the Indian; . . . He squats cross-legged in a circle with them, or at night around the fire, for two or three hours or even longer, all absorbing, forgetting aught else, discoursing to them with great serenity and deliberation; and though the food of the Indians is as nasty and disgusting as their dirty selves, the padre eats it with great gusto, and says that it is appetising and very nice. In fine, God has created him, I am sure, totally on purpose to hunt up these unhappy, ignorant and boorish people.

Garcés records in the diary, which he kept of his journeys, that he was the first *Español* to visit the land of the Mojave Indians.[2]

Whenever the priest went among the Indians he had with him a canvas print which showed on one side the picture of the Virgin Mary and the Infant Jesus. On

---

[1] Elliott Coues, translator and editor, *On the Trail of a Spanish Pioneer: The Diary and Itinerary of Francisco Garcés* (2 vols.; New York, 1900), p. 172 fn. Another edition of this diary, translated by John Galvin, was published under a revised title, San Francisco, 1965.   [2] *Ibid.*, p. 229.

the other side was the image of a "lost soul." The Indians liked the picture of the Virgin and the Baby, but
thought the one of the lost soul was very bad.

Garcés had been with Anza in 1774 when the
latter led an expedition from Sonora to San Gabriel
Mission, a few miles east of today's Los Angeles. The
old mission still stands near a town named for it in
Southern California. Anza had used the southern route
to reach San Gabriel. The expedition had to do with
the placing of a colony near San Francisco Bay. When
another expeditionary force was formed in 1775 for
the march to the mission, Garcés was scheduled to go
along. However when the march started he was left
behind on the Gila River.

With Garcés was another priest, several Indian servants and Sebastián Taraval, an Indian who had been
with Anza in 1774 as an interpreter. It was while Garcés
was with the Mojave Indians in rancherias near what is
today's Needles, California, that the priest stated his
desire to visit the "padres by the sea" at the San Gabriel
Mission.

The Mojaves told Garcés that they knew of the white
men at the mission and offered to guide him to it. The
priest refused the offer, giving for his reason that he was
low on supplies, but on his return from San Gabriel
would again visit the "Jamajabs," his name for the
Mojaves.

During his ministry in the Southwest, Garcés made
several trips throughout the region, studying the Indians,
their habits and problems, converting them to the Christian religion. He gave much time to those whom he

found ill with epidemics. This project is concerned only with the portion of his longest journey that brought him through new territory and led to his discovery of the Mojave River. Garcés was the first known white man to see the river and to follow it to its source, crossing the great sandy desert, later to be called the Mojave Desert. (It is possible, however, that Captain Pedro Fages saw the desert and was in some part of it in 1772 when he was searching for runaway Spanish soldiers. It was Fages who saw the Joshua trees and called them palms.)

On March 4, 1776, the little group made up of Garcés, three Mojaves and Sebastián set out on the journey to San Gabriel Mission. By March 6 they had traveled eight leagues when they came to a level, grassy spot where they found "small pines," which were doubtless cedars. They had reached the Providence Mountains. It was while camping there that four Indians came by and stopped to talk. They were returning from the coast where they had been trading in sea shells, which they prized. Garcés was surprised that they had no weapons with them on a route where there "was naught to eat, nor did they carry bows for hunting."[3] The traveling Indians replied that the "Jamajabs could endure hunger and thirst for four days." This was to tell the priest they were hardy men.

On the afternoon of March 7 Garcés took his party through a gap in the mountains which was bordered on both sides by sandhills. There he left the name Cañada de Santo Tomás to honor the apostle Thomas Didymus.

---

[3] *Ibid.*, p. 237.

They found no water at this point. The next day the little wayfaring group arrived at some very abundant wells. The priest named the wells Pozos de San Juan de Dios. They entered the Beñemé Indian nation at this site.

It was nearly one hundred years later that Dr. Elliott Coues visited the old watering-spot of Garcés which was still furnishing water in abundance. Dr. Coues, who was retracing Garcés' route, firmly believed the site of Marl Springs where he camped, was Garcés' Pozos de San Juan de Dios. Marl Springs was, for many years, the principal water camp between Rock Springs or Government Holes and the Sink of the Mojave River. Water was pumped consistently into watering troughs for cattle grazing in the area.

Garcés, who had words to spare for his Indian people, was laconic when it came to the entries in his diary. If he found grass, he stated the fact. If there was no water, he recorded just that much. There was no grumbling reported in his diary; no impatience shown.

Likewise, Garcés said nothing about the dun-colored landscapes being suddenly turned into a garden of exquisite wildflowers when spring arrived — which was the time of year when Garcés came through that area. There was no comment on the gold mat that lines the floor and sides of the washes and ravines in springtime. No mention of golden poppies on a hillside, nor the silver-gray desert holly that abounds. There was no ecstacy at a glimpse of a crimson blossom growing out of an earthless, waterless crack on a rocky hillside, far out of reach.

Daily, as he was making history over the uncharted region, he was not concerned about the appearance of the country. He arose with flaming dawns and camped in the beauty of the sunsets. He must have walked into purple mists along the river as winter turned into spring.

But always, Garcés was concerned with mileage, water, and grass. And ever thoughtful of his Indians.

5

Day of Discovery

The historic moment is always simple and brief;
it belongs to one man and one man alone,
without possibility . . of any confusion of rights.

William Bolitho,
from *Twelve against the Gods*

March 9, 1776, was the day of great moment in history. It was a day that might have been postponed many years in time and progress had it not been for the restless nature of Francisco Garcés who was so eager to seek a new route to the missions along the coast.

The river would have been found eventually, for of such is the unrolling of history. But Garcés, the patient padre of the Southwest Indians, was destined for the glory of the discovery of a river that stands alone in its uniqueness and importance. It was a connecting link in the chain of highways that brought civilization westward. The priest made history. He *was* history. However, that meant very little to the man who was dedicated to a life of converting savage Indians to the Christian faith. To Garcés the day meant progress in mileage. It meant grass and water. Those were the important finds of the day to him.

From his diary we find the following record:

March 9. I went 5 leagues (west) 1/4 west southwest, and arrived at a gap in the sierra that I named (Sierra)

Pinta for the veins that run in it of various colors. Here I
encountered an arroyo of saltish water that I named (Arroyo)
de los Mártires. There is good grass.[1]

That is all the discoverer had to say about a momentous happening almost two hundred years ago. He had
found the end of a river that was already a foot-trail
highway for a primitive race of people and a route which
was to become one of major importance to future generations. It was the season of the year that might have
found the river flowing with surplus water, but Garcés
made no mention of such.

On Font's map of 1777, the term "Arroyo de los
Mártires" appeared as the name of the Mojave River.
The same name had been applied to the Colorado River
in 1699 by Father Kino. This caused some confusion
through the early years.

The walls of Garcés' canyon are high and rocky. This
canyon was no doubt named in the early years of desert
travel, for a series of caves were eroded into the canyon.
For many yars it was called Cave Canyon. However, the
name now applied to it is Afton, and it is so marked
on the newer maps. The name Afton comes from the
name of the railroad station at the head of the canyon.
Also, the Cave Mountains in this region perpetuate the
former name of the ancient canyon.

One of the three caves formed over the ages was
destroyed when the Los Angeles and Salt Lake Railroad
(now owned by the Union Pacific Railroad) built its
tracks through the canyon. A five hundred and forty-two
foot tunnel was made to avoid going around the river

---

[1] Coues, *Diary of Garcés, op. cit.,* p. 238.

loop. It is said that part of the cave is still in existence, walled in by the wooden timbers of the lining of the tunnel. Al Proctor, now a resident of the Barstow area who was raised in the Afton region, says there is no top to the cave, and that it was destroyed when the railway entered the canyon.

The two remaining caves, formed side by side, are large enough to accommodate a dozen adult people, claims Dr. Edmund C. Jaeger, scientist who has made a thorough study of the canyon and the river. As they are the only natural shelters for miles around, it is quite possible that both white men and Indians used them for camp sites in the early days of travel. The roof of one of the caves is black with the soot of many campfires. The caves are fifteen feet deep and about as high.[2]

What sort of day did Garcés have on the day before his momentous discovery of an important waterway? Had there been any indication in the terrain of the country that might have given the priest an idea of the type of river he had come upon? What had been the hour of nightfall? Had the sun gone down early, with clouds hovering, or in a mist? Or had it gone softly over the rim of the sixty-five-square-mile playa they had crossed at the river's terminus? Was there a magnificent sunset, such as can be immeasurably beyond description on that far horizon? Was it a "just taken for granted" situation as the discoverer looked from Soda Lake's vast rim and turned onto Crucero Plain and entered the canyon with the pinkish walls?

---

[2] Edmund C. Jaeger, "The Upside Down River," in *Desert Magazine*, June 1957, p. 18.

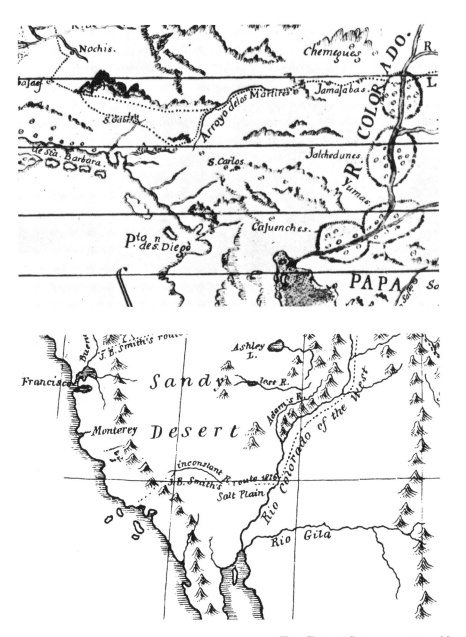

above: A portion of the Fr. Francisco Garcés map, 1777, showing the name as "Arroyo de los Mártires" as given by Garcés, and with the river ending in the desert.

below: A portion of the Albert Gallatin map, made in 1836 for the American Antiquarian Society. It shows the name as "inconstant R." (per Jedediah Smith); the river ending in the desert.

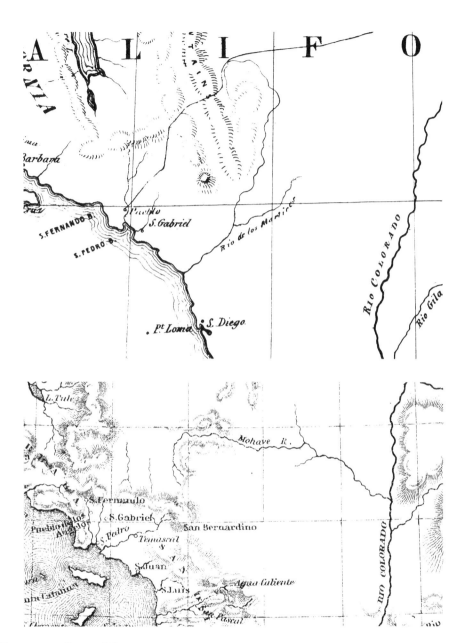

SHOWN ON EARLY MAPS

> *above:* A portion of the Rufus B. Sage map, 1846, showing the
> name as "R. de los Mártires," a wandering stream flowing to
> the Pacific Ocean near San Luis Rey.

> *below:* A portion of Lt. Charles Wilkes' map, 1849, drawn from
> Frémont's map; the "Mohave R." flows to the Colorado River.

Maps tend to show the Mojave River more accurately and with its present
name after the railroad surveys and Lt. Ives' report on the Colorado River,
both of the 1850s; however, a few maps of the early '50s were fairly
accurate.

What was the supper fare that evening? Dried meat? Wheat which they had brought with them from the Mojave Villages? Had they found the screw bean and mesquite with lingering dried pods still hanging on the trees near the water holes they had passed?[3] When they awakened the next morning what kind of a day was promised? Did the winds blow off the lake of crystalized chemicals that had been deposited there for millions of years? Did the bitter winds whip the bodies of the naked Indians? We shall probably never know the answers. All human reaction to this environment are reduced in the priest's diary to bare essentials — good grass, no grass, water, rain, food, the uncharted roads ahead, or leaving apt names for the campsites.

Was there a thought in Garcés' mind of what the river might do for a new country? For commerce, communication, or travel? Or was it something that reduced the miles, something to use as a pathmaker?

Garcés did note the colors in the rocky walls of the gorge, and he commented upon the taste of the water, and recorded that the grass was good.

There should have been wild game along the river and at the waterholes at that time of the year. One hundred and eighty-one years later, this writer went through that canyon and enjoyed a pastoral scene of great beauty and serenity. The Bighorn sheep were still coming down to drink of the Mojave waters in the

---

[3] The screw bean can be used in many ways — eaten green in the pods, ground into meal when dry, and the wood for fuel. Both the mesquite and screw bean are used for food for both humans and animals, by Indians and Mexicans. See Edmund C. Jaeger, *Desert Wild Flowers* (Stanford, 1968), pp. 93-96.

meadowland, and small animals were foraging for food while horses browsed on the grasslands.

Soda Lake is an outlet mostly in name in these later years. It is only in time of seasonal rains and melting snows that any water gets to the terminus, and there must be a rather large flood to bring it down in any great quantities.

The next day the Garcés' party arrived at a ranchería where the Indians (Beñemés) were so poor they had nothing to eat but the roots of rushes. There were "25 souls" at this stopping place. Garcés shared his "little store" with them, and they shared their rushes. Garcés' Indians did not care for the root diet.

It was raining and the Beñemés fussed because they could not go hunting for food. Garcés' picture of this group of Indians was not a pretty one. They were not only hungry, but they were naked. However, Garcés noted that they heard "with attention that which he told them of God."

On March 12 the missionary-priest and his four companions "halted" again on the river course at an uninhabited ranchería. It was still rainy and cold, and their hunger continued — they did not even have any roots for eating. Garcés had a horse killed and they stayed there until all the meat was gone. Not even the blood was wasted. From the site one of the Mojaves left Garcés to return to the Mojave Villages. The priest gave a blanket to one of the Indians, and to the other he gave a tunic (shirt).

One of Garcés' camps had been a site where the United States government was to build Camp Cady as a defense measure from hostile and thieving Indians. Elliott Coues went through the camp on his trip in 1865 and left a bleak picture of the installation for history. He called it a "God-forsaken Botany Bay" of a place. "The meanest I ever saw," he wrote; four officers and a handful of men were there in their mud and brush huts.

While crossing the river, Garcés' pack-mule mired down and everything that was on its back was wet so they tarried again. From this place he sent Sebastián and one of the Mojaves on ahead to search for another uninhabited ranchería. He took an observation and found their location to be at 34° 17'. Five Mojaves came along and stopped to talk; they had been to the coast for seashells.

Sebastián returned with the good news he had found a ranchería where he had been welcomed with kindness. By this time Garcés had taken another observation and found it to be below the thirty-fifth degree. He asked the Indians to take him westward which they refused to do, and no entreaties would change their decision. Garcés paused for a while at the ranchería Sebastián had found and they were well fed. They thought it delightful to become warm with food and kindness.

On March 19 the travelers stopped at the house of a "captain" and again were treated royally. The captain and his wife showered Garcés with seashells; the wife "tossed the basket" at him which was a sign of obeisance. They repeated their demonstration and the priest was very touched at the attention, for the shells were their prized possessions. The next day they stopped at another ranchería where there were seventy persons. They, too, gave Garcés a joyful welcome with shells, even showering his mule. At this point Garcés records that they were "near a gap betwen two cerros (hills) through which the river passes."

There has been some controversy through the years as to Garcés' route. The one going up the river into the San Bernardino Mountains, up Sawpit Canyon to the summit and descending the southern slope of the range by the ridge that lies west of Devil Canyon seems to be the accepted one among historians and students of the Garcés' route. Over this trail Garcés entered the San Bernardino Valley which he named St. Joseph because of its peacefulness.

Padre Garcés came and went into another phase of history, and except for his return to his southern desert post, he passes from these pages. Suffice it to say that Garcés passed this way; was a forerunner of a western civilization. He left a trail well marked in his diary, although it was to be fifty years before another white man broke a trail through the Mojave Desert.

About five years after the discovery of the Mojave River, Garcés died a martyr's death at the hands of Indians he had loved. It happened at the site on the Gila River where he was trying to establish a mission. The Indians lost all judgment in a misunderstanding of policy and murdered Garcés and three other priests along with the settlers.

Historians have retraced the Garcés' trail and have found definite reasons to believe that he either passed by or camped at such places we know today as the Barstow area, Oro Grande environs, Helendale, Victorville, and Hesperia.

The peaceful Indians of Garcés' time were later re-placed by warlike ones which, because of their hostility and horse-stealing, made later trails wretched for the passing emigrants and for the early settlers.

PART III

Links with Civilization

6

The Cajon Pass

Mountains are earth's undecaying monuments.

Nathaniel Hawthorne,
from *Sketches from Memory*

A familiar place name in California is "Cajon." This name has been applied to one of the important mountain passes in the state. The word is of Spanish origin, literally meaning "box." The name came into use because of the natural features of the box-like canyon that serves as a pass through the country between the Mojave Desert and the valleys that lie south and west of the desert rim.

The Cajon Pass is distinctively different from most mountain passes. It is not a pass between two mountains; it is a pass between two mountain ranges, and they overlap: the San Bernardino mountain range is to the east and the San Gabriel mountain range to the west. The latter is the older range.

Long years in the past, the pass became the "gateway to the wilds of the interior." What an interior it is! Coming to or going from the coastal area or the southern region of the state, that great mass of mountain peaks and sheer drops from the high precipices are startling and they culminate into one of the most rugged, as well as one of the most beautiful ranges, in the West.

Vast expanses of the mountain region have no use

other than for grazing. Even so, much of it is there for beauty. Those steep, almost straight up and down precipices make one think of the "vast forever," so boundless they appear to man.

The overlapping of the eastern end of the San Bernardino Mountains caused the forming of the pass, geologists tell us. In the pass area there is an alluvial deposit about two miles wide. A few miles above the Devore railway station the deposit narrows and becomes the Blue Cut (gorge) and it is here that the pass crosses over the San Andreas Rift. This area abounds with phenomena caused by the fault and has become a geologist's paradise.

The fact that this pass was at the western end of the Old Spanish Trail made it an important spot in the emigrant days. It was difficult to cross with wagons in those times. Today's specific Cajon Pass is not exactly the pass used in the days of the 'Forty-niners and the Mormons. The artifices of man's great earth moving machines have changed the route of the pass by rewinding the curves or eliminating them to such an extent that historic site locations are now only approximations.

Camp Cajon, three miles above the Blue Cut, was once an old Indian village. Here the pass becomes wider, a fan-shaped site bounded by the divide on the upper edge. The divide is the desert rim. Eroding water caused the formation of two major divisions which are known as East and West Cajon. They are separated by a ridge of more solid formation that stretches downward from the desert rim.

The railroad and the highway—and now the freeway —run through East Cajon. Until a paved road was completed through West Cajon, this valley with a level floor was little known. Peaks as high as five thousand feet rise in the mountains that run about ten miles along the pass. The south slope is very steep in the West Cajon area. These deep gaps have served as crossings for man at some time. The most easterly of the crossings into the Cajon is now called Summit Station. This is the site where the Old Spanish Trail passed.

The average traveler of today takes the beautiful road in stride, with little thought of the vigorous days when this region was frightening to the traveler, with its tall rocky mountains, and the little valleys that look so inviting as well as terrifying below such steepness.

Long before the Cajon pathway was an accepted one and used freely, the wilderness of the Cajon region was a hide-out for renegade white men and Indians. Cattle and horse stealing became so common that the people of the lower valleys had to take to battle. Once in the interior of the vast area beyond Cajon, it was almost impossible to recover the animals.

Horse-thieving was worse than the stealing of cattle, as horses were easier to handle in droves. The thieves ran rampant for years, making it very difficult for the stockmen. The caravans which made the trip through the country between New Mexico and California were on the alert for the robbers, for they were an open invitation with the droves of horses they took over the trail.

At one time a contingent from the Mormon Battalion was placed on guard at Cajon to aid in putting a stop to the stock-stealing thieves. Battles were fought, sometimes by posses formed among the ranchers and stockmen and with enlisted aid from San Bernardino.

In the late 1840s the Mormons came into California, cruising their way over the high passes into San Bernardino Valley, and finding ways through the mountainous country of the Cajon area where they could best take their wagons over passes.

The Mormons were not attracted by the gold to the north as much as for territories that would let them get a foothold for grass-roots living. It was part of their personal gospel to prove their faith by their ways of living, and always the church was uppermost in a good Mormon's life. They did much to promote the travel lines in the uncharted country. The Mormons sometimes came with large parties, and at other times small groups wended their way over the steep grades. The small parties often ran into trouble.

One pioneer, S. N. Carvalho, an American in spite of his European name, came over the country in 1854. He was an artist and had an eye for the beauty that most of the emigrants failed to see. In his journal telling of the trip he wrote: "The view from the top of the pass is grand beyond description." It was indeed unusual for an emigrant to write about the beauties of the region. They were mainly intent on passing over all that beauty which seemed to them nothing but a barrier to their comfort and their lives.

The railroad companies had their eyes on Cajon Pass during the years of the opening of the West. Many verbal battles were fought by the rival railways. Land surveying began in the 'sixties. Before that, land was measured by metes and bounds. Often the date of the survey was cut into tree trunks if the tree had been used as a marker. These were called witness trees.

One of the historic roads built in 1861 was the John Brown Toll Road. It was established to connect the desert with the outside world. John Brown, Sr., was a man of great activity and spent a long life helping the desert to advance. When San Bernardino was made a county he was one of the first legislators. He had been a member of Frémont's expedition at one time. His Toll Road was twelve miles long and was a vital link in the progress of the desert country. With Henry Willis and George L. Tucker of San Bernardino, Brown secured a twenty-year franchise for operating the road. The road came through Cajon Pass to the floor of the desert and connected with the Van Dusen Road built from Holcomb Valley to the desert. After operating the Toll Road for eighteen years, Brown leased it out for the two remaining years. Afer that the road became a free county road.

John Brown, Sr., was a colorful character. He was a miner, cattleman, road builder, and tireless in his activities in building for the desert's future. He lived to a good old age. He had ten children; four of them were boys who, in maturity owned land in the desert.[1]

---

[1] Ellsworth A. Sylvester, *Mohahve, No. II* (Mohahve Historical Society, 1964).

7

Indians of the Desert

We will give the name of our fearless race
To each bright river whose course we trace.

Felicia D. Hemans,
from *Song of Emigration*

Forty-three years after Father Garcés had crossed the Mojave Desert, there were still no white men living upon it. There were Indians; some of them were roving nations following weather conditions or food supplies. Many were warlike; others were peaceful.

The Mojave Indians lived in the Colorado River region as they did in Garcés' time; however, they were not as peaceful as they had been when Garcés walked among them. Many had long since reverted to the way of living in war or peace that was theirs before Father Garcés had worked with them.

There were no missions at any time on the Mojave Desert. However, Christian Indians now and then drifted into the desert region; some were renegade Indians who had run away from the missions on the coast. There were others who came to live peacefully. The Mojaves, whom Garcés had loved so well, came up from the Colorado to make war upon the peaceful ones, and sometimes on the Indians who had accepted Christianity.

The Mojaves who lived on the shores of the Colorado River had a better way of life than most of the nations of the Southwest. The Colorado River outpoured much of its waters in annual spring floods, enriching the lands near its banks. The Mojaves had learned the art of raising vegetables. They knew how to construct houses of mud and sticks, and they were skilled in pottery making and basketry.

Occasionally Indian tribes warred amongst themselves, but as a rule neighboring nations were friendly toward one another. The Yumas and Mojaves were notably aggressive to outsiders.

From a very interesting old report of an expedition led by Lieutenant Gabriel Moraga in November 1819 to punish the Mojave Indians, we have the word picture of the combined soldiery and the Church in attempting to halt depredations on both Christian and pagan Indians. The report is recorded in the diary of Father Joaquin Nuez, chaplain of the expedition.

Lieutenant Moraga was the outstanding explorer and Indian fighter of his time, as was his father before him, when he had assisted Anza in settling Monterey. The name Moraga is a distinguished one in the history of California.

The report[1] of the 1819 expedition is narrated in a form of writing so detailed that one sentence of the opening paragraph takes eighteen lines of a typed sheet of letter paper. The present chronicler of the expedition's entry into the Mojave Desert must give it much less drama than the diarist used. He wrote, in part:

---

[1] "Moraga Expedition, November-December 1819," Santa Barbara Archives (Bancroft Library), tomo IV, pp. 137-49: diary of Fr. Joaquin Pascual Neuz, minister of San Gabriel and chaplain of the expedition.

. . . the Indians of the Rancheria of Amajaba (Mohaves) have the audacity to come and commit deeds of violence on the pagan Indians of the Rancheria of Atongaibit[2] and the others of the region, and the Christians who had fled from the Mission of San Fernando and the one of San Gabriel.

As the son of obedience that I am, I begin:

From this interesting old record we find that the military force traveled to the desert, going south of the "Cajon of Amusopiabit," about nine leagues distant from Cucamonga Ranch, to punish murdering Mojaves.

Throughout the recorded events, the chaplain complained about the bitter cold weather. They passed the Cajon "in spite of a large rough hill" and arrived about noon at what is today's Las Flores Ranch, then called Ranchería of Guapiabit, about nine and a half leagues from Cajon Pass. The expeditionary force rested at the lovely pastoral site for the sake of both men and animals. Their next stop was at the Ranchería of Atongaibit, where at that time there was a large swamp. The Mojaves had killed several Indians — four Christians from San Gabriel Mission, three from San Fernando, and some pagans. Expedition members buried the bones of the Indians who had been murdered by the Mojaves and gave a Catholic burial service for the Christian Indians. The chaplain renamed the site "Blessed Souls of Atongaibit."[2]

The expedition had started from San Gabriel Mission in November. In the entry for December 2, the chaplain recorded that the commanding officer (Moraga) who

[2] *Ibid.*, Rancheria Atongaibit was located a short distance above present-day Victorville, and adjacent to present-day Hesperia.

had received the information that water was scarce except for one day's journey before reaching the Mojave settlement, decided to send ten soldiers and four Indians ahead of the expedition to scout for water and grass. At this point Nuez wrote that Lieutenant Moraga was "heartsick because he was unable to proceed further" because their horses were giving out from lack of feed and "even water for all the animals of the expedition."

The next day when the commander decided to turn back to the Ranchería of San Joaquin and Santa Ana of Angayaba; they met quite a number of Indians, including children of various ages, and saw many dead bodies of Indians. They could not find all the reported Indians who had been disturbed by enemies. They regretted they could not "proceed to Amajaba."

On December 7, the expedition started back to the mission and stopped at San Hilario. Rain added to the chill of the winter days and nights. Many were ill from the affects of the weather. The diarist complained "he who writes this suffered more than anyone else, because of not having the equipment customary for riding constantly in campaigns, for he bore arms, and rode in some thin old trousers of nankin so that he is suffering in the right leg and wrist."

Having left San Gabriel on November 22, they had been gone twenty-two days. They stopped again at Cucamonga. The commander sent the troops and the animals on to the mission because the grass was scarce on the "land of the Puente Rancho."

"Said Señor and I spent the night at the Puente," Nuez wrote, and the next day they arrived at San Gabriel Mission "from the struggle."

The expedition had accomplished nothing, and the poor chaplain probably never got warm. He was very bitter over the march and was cold day and night. According to him, almost everyone in the force was in the same state of mind.

"This land is most sterile," he included in his report. ". . . in proof of this, in all the road not a bird was encountered, nor even hardly a worm. If another time it is thought necessary to punish to Mojaves, I am of the opinion. . ." The unhappy priest went on in detail describing how he would plan the next expedition, so there would be help at certain places, horses and men, hay and water. He would have tanks, "wide and sufficiently deep," dug in the earth to hold reserve water. His theory was fine. He advised that the expedition be planned for a warmer season. Three horses for each individual should be sent on ahead. Two months ahead of time, pack loads of the "indispensable" things, such as "ammunition, canons, food stuffs, in order that thus, without any confusion, within a few days, the perverse Mojaves may speedily learn the power of God and of our arms."

It seems incredible that a whole expeditionary force could march along the Mojave River and not be aware that there was water somewhere near. To pass through the Las Flores area with the West Fork of the Mojave River flowing through the meadows, and not see some sign of water from its tributaries or the river itself, is strange. November rains should have brought some water to the surface.

There is an interesting point that might well be considered here: On an earlier expedition, in 1816, the bones of three children had been found somewhere between Victorville and Barstow. The commander of the expedition gave the name "San Hilario" to the area where the children's bones were found.

We know that Garcés crossed the desert in 1776; that Father José Zalvidea had been near Hesperia and Victorville in 1809 baptising Indians. The expedition of 1816 when the children were buried, and the later expedition in 1819, show that there were white men in the Mojave Desert four times before Jedediah Smith came through in 1826. True, all of them did not completely cross the Mojave Desert. True again, none of the four preceding Smith were Americans.

During the years that followed the settling of the desert, with its passing parade of emigrants, and the caravans trailing their last sinuous trips between New Mexico and Los Angeles, with the 'Forty-niners and the Mormons and their wagons widening the trails, the Indians were actively stealing stock from the ranches and from emigrants bringing their stock into California.

Michael White was given in 1843 a grant of land at the mouth of Cajon Pass—the Rancho Muscupiabe. White was an Englishman by birth but had been naturalized as a Mexican and was entitled to receive a grant. He suggested, when he asked for the grant, that he might be able to help ward off the cattle and horse thieves if he built a house on the site of his ranch. The house was built to the west of the mouth of what is known today as Cable Canyon. It overlooked both Cajon Pass and the Mojave Trail. He thought a ranch there would be an obstacle to the Indians who were stealing the stock and hiding it in the interior country. Instead of being a help, White had his own stock stolen. He had to abandon the ranch, and the trail was again open to the invaders.

While posses, settlers, and army contingents were trying to patrol the Cajon Pass area to protect it from hostile Indians and horse thieves, there was similar activity in the lower river valley near the terminus of the Mojave River. Help had been sent from Fort Tejon as a temporary measure. The United States government had Camp Cady set up as a fort for protection of the settlers and the emigrants.

The shelters at Camp Cady were made of mud and brush. The quarters were squalid and miserable. The quality of the horses was poor, and usually an animal was good on the patrol and escort work for no more than six months.

In 1868, after the Civil War was over, the fort at Cady was moved about a mile west. There was level ground at the new site and a drill field could be made. Some of the soldiers deserted. The isolation and lack of any recreation was hard on the troops. As a rule, the fort was poorly manned and at times the number of officers and troops was low. After the war, a number of forts and redoubts were established between Las Vegas (then known as Vegas Spring) and Camp Cady. Camp Cady was named for Albermarle Cady, a military officer.

In 1870, General Price from Fort Mohave (Arizona), held a conference with the Indians and peace terms were reached. Camp Cady was abandoned and the property was sold to stockmen.

The ruins of the old camp and water hole lay idle a long time, disintegrating from the wind and floods. A plaque was placed at the site in 1966 by E. Clampus Vitus, an historical group.

8

Mojave's Explorers

On sands and shores and desert wildernesses.
John Milton, from *Samson Agonistes*

About fifty years after Garcés discovered the Mojave River, won his martyr's crown, and attained his place in history, America began to feel growing pains, although she was very young as nations measure their time. De Anza had made a settlement at Monterey. There had been some travel to the Northwest. The Spanish had left a heritage in the Southwest. But the Mojave country, with its underground river seeping slowly through the desert valley, lay waiting.

Jedediah Strong Smith, a New Yorker, who had already won a fine reputation as an explorer and trapper, came down from the Salt Lake country. He made two trips into California's desert region. Historians are not in full agreement regarding the two Smith entries into the Mojave Desert, and through the Cajon. Many are convinced he followed the old Garcés trail into the San Bernardino Mountains and into the valley below. He was the first white man to explore the Mojave Desert. Garcés, Zalvidea, and the Mojave-punishing military company under the leadership of Gabriel Moraga, preceded Smith, although they did no exploring.

Smith did for California what Lewis and Clark accomplished for the Northwest. His is the distinction of being the first American to cross the Mojave Desert, and the first to cross the Sierra Nevada range of mountains. He first entered the Mojave country in 1826. It is evident from his journal entries that he was following the old Garcés Trail. He had Indian guides as had Garcés.

Smith's party had entered California to survey the beaver trapping possibilities. The trip was both eventful and tragic. They ran into difficulties — they were so near starvation that they ate their own horses, which were also starving. Smith took his men to the San Gabriel Mission where they were received kindly by the fathers. However, they had trouble with the Mexican authorities. American sea captains went to his aid and he was released with an order to return the way he had entered California.

Smith disregarded the order and went up through the San Joaquin Valley where he left his furs and managed to get through the Sierra Nevada range to the annual rendezvous in the Salt Lake region. In 1827 he went back through the desert to gather his men and the rest of his furs. He made better time on the trail as he knew the way. The Mojaves were not as friendly as they had been in Garcés' time, and they turned on the white men and killed ten of them. Smith and the remaining men fled from the Indians and again stopped at San Gabriel Mission. The same governor detained them, but again American seamen helped him out of an expected prison sentence. He left with his men and horses for the Northwest, taking his furs.

Of one of his trips Smith wrote in his journal, "I then proceeded . . . until I got near the head of the

Inconstant River . . . instead of traveling southeast around the bend of the stream, I struck directly
across the plain nearly s.s.w. to the gap in the mountain."

Smith, who had crossed the Mojave River at or near
Oro Grande, was impressed with the hide-and-seek quali-
ties of the stream as it rose from under the surface and
dipped suddenly out of sight. So the Mojave River had
another name. After Smith's journeys into the desert,
the name "Inconstant" appeared on many of the early
maps.

Smith made it through the Cajon area, but historians
cannot definitely determine which canyon he followed
among the many that cut into the mountain ranges that
overlap and reach out with yawning gaps.

The Beattie book[1] records that Smith's route in 1826
took him over the Old Mojave Trail out of the San
Bernardino Mountains and down into the San Bernardino Valley. The Beatties also record that an Indian
guide, with Smith on the second trip, "testified that they
took the route by Otongallavil," which was an Indian
village on the Mojave Desert where the trail to the
San Joaquin led from the Mojave Trail. It was near
Hesperia.

Smith's expeditions through the Mojave Desert were
rough. He was quite a young man when he started on
his western adventures as a trapper and explorer. He
was a very religious person. He was still young when
he was killed by Comanche Indians in 1831 on the
Cimarron Desert.

It was nearly twenty years before another explorer

---

[1] Beattie, *Heritage of the Valley*, pp. 21-24.

and trailblazer came into the Mojave Desert. While searching for the Old Spanish Trail, John C. Frémont, military pathmaker for the United States government, was following the Mojave River.

Frémont had a very expressive command of the English language and, as he was interested in the desert for its oddities, he wrote a great deal about it for the government records as well as for his family. Many of his writings about the West were published in eastern newspapers, and it was no doubt partly due to the extravagant descriptions he sent back to the East that many people came west. He was interested in the plant life of the West and gathered specimens to send or take back east for recording. One time he lost a thousand of these when a mule fell into a chasm.

While Frémont was in camp one day (near what is now Barstow) six Indians came by and stopped to talk. Five of them were Mojaves. The one who was not a Mojave had been educated in a Spanish mission and spoke English well. Frémont recorded the name Mojave as it sounded to him, spelling it "Mohahve," and later entered it on his maps as the Mohahve River. The Indians told him that the Mojaves had lived along this river (where the camp was located) long ago. The visiting Indians lived on the Colorado River in Frémont's time. From his conversation with these passing Indians, Frémont received a hint of the history of the Mojave Indians of an earlier era, and thought it would be worthwhile to learn of that past era.

Scientist Edmund C. Jaeger gives credence to the pathfinder's statement in recording what the educated

Indian told him of the Mojaves who formerly lived along "this river." Frémont did record the words of the Indian interpreter and it is quite possible the Indians did refer to centuries of the past. Dr. Jaeger writes:

> From archaeological evidence we are led to believe that from the tenth to the sixteenth century A.D. there was a branch of the Mohave people living to the westward along the borders of Soda Lake and other waters ponded in lakes along the course of the Mohave River (Cronise Lake, Lake Manix), all in what is now eastern San Bernardino County. Charred heaps of clam shells left in the bordering sands and fire-blackened stones along the old beach lines mark the sites of their camps. When encroaching aridity made the area unfavorable for further occupancy, they withdrew and settled alongside their more favorably situated brothers in the Colorado River bottomlands. But as late as 1776, Father Garcés, the early Spanish missionary, found Mohave still occupying some territory a considerable distance to the west of Soda Lake, also along the Lower Mohave River.[2]

In 1853 Lieutenant R. S. Williamson was sent out by the government to map one of the routes for a possible railroad between the Mississippi River and the Pacific Coast. Reaching the San Joaquin Valley, Williamson dropped south and skirted the northern slope of the San Gabriel Mountains to the Mojave Desert, following the Mojave River to its mouth at Soda Lake.

Frémont might have been the one to discover the fact but Williamson proved beyond a doubt that the Mojave River ended at Soda Lake, rather than flowing into the Colorado River as many explorers and travelers firmly believed. Even Frémont's cartographer, Charles Preuss,

---

[2] Edmund C. Jaeger, *The California Deserts* (Stanford, 1965), pp. 115-16.

in 1848, showed the Mojave River flowing to the Colorado.

It is to be noted that Mojave's type of river is signified by the expression, "It ends at Soda Lake." An ordinary river would "empty into Soda Lake."

PART IV

On the Trail

9

Mormon Trailways

*It seemed the Lord
fitted the back for the burden!*

Wallace Stegner,
from *The Gathering of Zion*[1]

The Mormons, known officially as the Church of Jesus Christ of Latter-day Saints, had been having a difficult time in the eastern and central states in the first half of the nineteenth century. Starting from a vision their prophet Joseph Smith claimed to have received, this faith was based on golden plates which Smith discovered and translated. This new church had a dedicated following. The practice of polygamy set other religious faiths against them, eventually leading to misunderstandings and even persecutions.

Before these people had settled down in Utah to build an empire, there had been hundreds of them on the trails west. The Mojave River Valley had its share. They came across the Great American Desert. They traveled in wagons. They walked to lighten loads. They pushed handcarts across half a continent. They came by way of the Northwest. They went around the Horn in ships and then went east to Utah. They went in boats up the Mississippi from New Orleans and crossed the wide

---

[1] Quoted with permission of the publisher, McGraw Hill Book Co.

Missouri. They came from foreign countries to join the swelling numbers of Latter-day Saints.

The Mormons settled briefly in Ohio, Missouri, Illinois, and Iowa after they left New York state. They built a temple, homes, and business structures in Nauvoo, Illinois, and it was in Illinois that their first leader was murdered. Persecutions followed them wherever they went, and along the lonely trails. They opened civilization in many places, and caused those communities to prosper as they farmed, and were ready at a moment's notice to pick up what they could and move on to wherever their leaders directed.

The new leader, Brigham Young, eventually chose a place for his people — the valley of the Great Salt Lake. There they started their empire that in the coming years was to spread over the nation. There are no definite physical boundaries; but the boundary lines are wherever Mormons gather — in their hearts, homes and work.

The movement of the Mormons on the trail was organized so that most of the groups knew where the others were. The opportunity came for the Mormons to form a battalion of soldiers to aid in the war with Mexico. The idea developed either in the ranks of the Mormons, through their enemies, or with the federal government.

Young approved the idea, either because of the fact that he was using good judgment to keep in favor with the United States, or for the actual financial assistance that would go with it. Money was scarce with the Mormons at that time, and Young was aware that not only would the soldiers be moved at government expense, but that a certain percentage of the soldiers' pay would revert to the church. It was a wonderful march the Mormon Battalion made — two thousand miles, walking all the way, pulling wagons over the rough ground, through all kinds of disagreeable weather, and meeting other obstacles. Their commander, Colonel Philip St. George Cooke, praised them greatly when they reached San Diego and found the war was over. Some of the soldiers re-enlisted, but others scattered through Southern California seeking work to earn money to return to Utah and their families. Some of them were in central California at the time gold was discovered.

The soldiers who remained in the southern part of the state were attracted to the San Bernardino Valley. They had never known such climate; it seemed to be a wonderful place for a Mormon colony. Captain Jefferson Hunt, who had been an officer in the Battalion, started scouting about for an ideal place for a colony and worked hard to get the Mormon leaders to see it that way.

Hunt had occasion to make a trip back to California after returning home, and he knew something of the trail conditions. In 1849 he led a large train of pioneers through from Utah to Los Angeles. That was the trip on which a number of people defected from the trail and found themselves in Death Valley.

Two years later, a wagon train was brought to California for settling a colony. The place that Hunt had found and which was available for the Mormons, was the Chino Land Grant (near the later towns of Ontario and Pomona). It was owned by Isaac Williams, an American who became a naturalized Mexican, and so could obtain a grant. The ranch was expansive and delightful with broad pastures and great trees for shade and beauty. It could accommodate a large number of families. Williams, who was always hospitable and kind to the emigrants, offered to sell his holdings.

The wagon train that left Utah consisted of four hundred and fifty people. They brought stock with them — horses, mules, cattle. They traveled in parties — ten wagons to a company — and were to gather at a place called Sycamore Grove below Cajon Pass, near the Devore Cut-off. It was a motley group with representation from every state in the Union except two. Mormons from Canada, England, Wales, Ireland, Australia, Sweden and France were in the colony.

The Mormon leaders left the families in camp while they went to complete negotiations at the Williams Ranch. They were greeted with the news that the owner had doubled the price he had been asking; then he changed his mind again and refused to sell. While the campers started living their community camp life, the leaders sought another site. It proved to be the Lugo Grant, now including the city of San Bernardino. The colony, started in 1851, was recalled by Young to Utah six years later. In the meantime the trail through the Mojave River Valley had become a highway for traffic. Thousands of wagons came through the desert.

The Mojave River was always a welcome sight to the emigrants. No matter how tough the trail had been, when they reached the river they were sure of water, grass for the stock, and time for rest.

On the long trail westward there had been a great deal of suffering. They had learned the grace of patience and the strength of fortitude. They were often hungry.

The weather could be dreadful. But they had the strength of their ambitions.

Quite a number of the emigrants kept journals of their trail life. From those, future generations have learned of the trials — the suffering, the illnesses, the fear of Indians, the loss of stock, and death. Many a family horse that had hauled wagons through heavy sand and waterless area, had to be shot to end its suffering. There were steep mountain grades where the emigrants had to get out and walk uphill to ease the load for the animals.

All the passing emigrants helped to develop the river valley, for there were many who liked the desert and settled along the Mojave River. From such camps grew settlements, and finally towns.

10

Historic Springs

Rest and be Thankful.

William Wordsworth

Water was the most essential ingredient of the western trails. How welcome were the natural springs that flowed from the rocks and mountainsides of the desert, where one would least expect such a miracle. Such opportune locations were far apart — often as much as sixty miles between waterholes or springs. But the wonder of being privileged to come upon a clear, cool spring! To have a drink of fresh, sweet water instead of the dregs of a rusty keg! To be able to cook with the fresh water which made the everlasting beans taste better. To be able to wash off the dust and grime of the trail — to have clean hands, faces, and to be able to bathe their bodies and wash their clothing. It made the clean, limp sunbonnets look like Easter hats.

One of those heaven-sent oases was Marl Springs. Dr. Elliott Coues (translator of the Garcés diary, and who retraced the priest's route in 1865) stopped at Marl Springs to camp. The caravan trail of the New Mexican merchants who traveled annually (to Los Angeles in the fall, and back to Santa Fe in the spring) made use of the springs that seemed like the miraculous pitcher of myth. There the long pack train of animals, drovers, and servants, could be refreshed.

In 1862, John Brown, Sr., who built the toll road from Cajon Pass to the Mojave River, and then later, went to Needles to construct a ferry over the Colorado River, made use of Marl Springs. He recorded the trips in a diary. He found the road to be very poor and often had to leave his wagon and go on ahead, sending back later for the wagon. He filled kegs with the water from the plenteous spring. In later years, the spring was used for the cattle that grazed in the area.

Resting Springs, located in the southeastern tip of Inyo County, was an important stop for the travelers of the early days. Here was an abundance of clear water, a welcome and enjoyable sight for thirsty people whose tongues and mouths became constricted from the dust and wind, and their throats parched. The tired, patient animals, jaded from pulling the wagons through heavy sand and uneven gravel, could rest and browse and build up their strength on the tender grass. Resting Springs is not far from today's Tecopa. The name is still in use.

While Frémont and his party were camped in the vicinity of the Mojave River near where Barstow is today, two Mexicans, a man named Andres Fuentes, and an eleven-year-old boy, Pablo Hernendes, approached camp. They belonged to a small party of six who were driving thirty horses to New Mexico. They had first chosen to go ahead of the annual caravan so as to find better feed and water for the animals. However, they had suddenly decided to connect with the caravan on the Old Spanish Trail as they felt fear for their safety.

A few days before, they had been visited by a group of Indians who seemed very friendly. Then they returned in great numbers and charged upon the small camp with blood-thirsty yells and flying arrows. The others in the camp were Fuentes' wife, Pablo's parents, and Santiago Giacome, the leader of the party. At the time the Indians appeared Fuentes and Pablo had been guarding the horses and Giacome shouted to them to drive the animals away which they did. They drove them to a spring (later to be called Bitter Springs) and left the horses, taking off to find a camp somewhere, or to meet the caravan. They found the Frémont camp and told their story. Frémont offered to help them find the horses and to go back and find the other members of the group.

The Americans took to the trail and went northward through a bad stretch of country. There was a scarcity of trees, and the desert plain was strewn with rocks that were destructive to the soft-footed animals. Now and then they came upon a meager stream or a waterhole. They found wildflowers, presenting an ironic picture to the bleakness of the land. When they reached the site where Fuentes had left the horses, they were gone.

Frémont made camp at the stop and asked for volunteers to continue the search for the people and animals. Only Kit Carson and Alex Godey volunteered. That evening Fuentes returned to the camp saying his horse had given out. In the afternoon of the following day Carson and Godey returned to camp with two bloody scalps dangling from Godey's gun and some of the horses which Fuentes recognized. They had a story to tell.

The two men had followed the trail by moonlight until late in the night, as the moon was brilliant and lighted the way. When the trail took them through a narrow defile, they fastened their horses securely and lay down to sleep. When daylight came they took up the trail. They came upon an Indian camp, fastened their horses, and took a position where they could look down on the Indians. Because of movement among the horses, the scouts were discovered. The men charged upon them with their own war shouts and a steady rain of shots. They did not know how many Indians might be in the large tents. Two Indians fell. The scouts stripped off the scalps and captured a small boy. Suddenly, one of the "dead Indians" sprang to his feet, a horrible sight with blood streaming from his head. An old squaw, thought by the scouts to be the mother of the revived Indian, stopped on her way in following the fleeing Indians up a hill, turned and shook her fists at the scouts. One of the scouts, appalled at the sight of the wounded Indian, put him out of his misery.

The camp site of the Indians was a fine one, with water spouting from a spring in the mountainside. The camp showed that preparations had been made for a big feast. They must have been expecting a crowd for there was a basket filled with about fifty moccasins. Great earthen vessels, filled with horse meat, were set over fires. A number of fine animals had been slaughtered for the feast. The boy showed no grief at the situation. He sat, tied up, chewing on a horse head for his breakfast.

Godey had received an arrow through his collar, which barely missed his neck.

Fuentes said they were about fifty miles from the next campsite and they left that night, expecting to travel all night. Guided by Fuentes, they started out over the desert. It was April, but Frémont wrote of the intense heat. They found skeletons of horses along the trail which took them through a canyon now known as Red Pass, and past Silver Lake, which is beyond the terminus of the Mojave River. They traveled over dreadfully rough country. Finally, they dropped down on a sandy plain where there was a verdant spot with springs and bushes. That was the Archilete. It was a delightful spot, peaceful and quiet—too much so.

They found the bodies of the two mutilated men—Giacome and Hernendes—but there was no sign of the two women. Sadly it was considered that the Indians had taken them. Pablo's little dog was there, frantic with joy to see the boy. Whatever compunction the members of Frémont's party felt about the scalped-alive Indian ceased.

More history was enacted at Bitter Springs. The story is told of an elderly Mexican named Meso, called Tio (uncle) because of his advanced age. His party was so full of joy to find water (as they had been practically dying of thirst) that they decided to celebrate. They dressed in their best and prepared food. They sang and danced all evening. But poor Tio Meso dropped dead from a stroke. For a time the springs were called Agua del Tio Meso for the elderly man. It is thought that Captain Jefferson Hunt gave the name Bitter to the springs when he was escorting the 1849 wagon train through from Salt Lake to Los Angeles.

In a private party, led by the father of western-famed Wyatt Earp, a group of people from as far east as Kentucky, came through the Mojave Desert. The wife of Dr. J. A. Rousseau kept a diary of the long trail trip. This party crossed the country in 1864. By the time they reached Bitter Springs they were out of food, and in bad shape from lack of water. Help was sent to them from Camp Cady. Mrs. Rousseau's diary told much about the trail and the people in the train. She spoke of the high-tempered Mr. Earp and the fact that people could not get along with him. Several members of the group, she wrote, left him and asked to join the Rousseau party. She wrote sadly of the fate of two family horses — the mare, Fan, that had to be shot to be relieved of suffering, and the good horse Charlie which it seemed would share the same fate.

About thirty miles north of Baker is the site of Salt Springs where gold was found along the trail in the early years. Members of Mormon parties also discovered gold, but there was no opportunity to take any interest in the discovery. Some years later development started in gold mining and for about a century, according to L. Burr Belden, desert historian, the mines continued to operate. There was a great deal of Indian trouble in the region and often the mines had to stop operating. In 1846, the Amargosa Mining Company was active at Salt Springs. Once, when only eight men were at the mines, Paiute Indians attacked them. One man got away to get help — having to travel forty-five miles to reach the military post at Marl Springs, from where help was sent. When the soldiers reached Salt Springs, the seven men were dead, not knowing that the messenger had gotten through and that help was on the way.

PART V

Settlements of the
Mojave River Valley

11

Ranch of the Flowers

*Let the fields and the guiding streams
in the valley delight me. Inglorious,
let me court the rivers and forests.*

Virgil, from *Georgics*

Beautiful Las Flores Ranch lies peacefully in a fertile river valley through which the West Fork of the Mojave idles its way over the meadowlands upon which cattle have grazed for a century. In the foothills, the West Fork and Deep Creek have become one stream — the Mojave. Surrounding the large and famous ranch are rugged mountains, towering high over craggy hills, deep ravines, and shaded canyons. The peaceful Afton-type river has met few tributaries, but it picks up the run-off waters from the mountain slopes and the Cedar Springs region.

The waters that reach the valley have enriched it and it has always been prosperous.

The summer sun pours down on the strong, bright land that glistens with countless grains of sand. Spring makes it a pastoral valley, but in summer, it broods as the cattle browse. Men ride over the range — and have done so for fully a century. In the fall of the year the winds murmur and the trees quiver. In the winter the winds blow cold over the vast acreage. But life on the ranch has always been active. Cattle have browsed over a thousand hills and knolls, and drifted to higher areas where pasturage was leased to the cattle range of Las Flores.

The ranch has a history other than that of grazing cattle. It lies in the path of an old Indian trail of long ago, connecting the inner regions with coastal areas. Father Garcés followed Indian guides over this slope of the mountains, through Holcomb and Bear valleys (up Sawpit Canyon) to reach the summit, and went down into San Bernardino Valley. From there, Garcés plodded on and was soon with his friends, "the padres by the sea," whom he was so eager to visit at San Gabriel Mission.

Father José Zalvidea came through the region to bless the Indians at the little village of Guapiabit (now near the ranch headquarters), and expeditionary forces crossed the land on the way to the country of the Mojaves who had murdered both Christian and pagan Indians on the desert.

At one time the ranch site was considered a good location for an army defense post to check the depradations of horse-thieving Indians as they swept over the coastal valley grazing lands and drove away stock belonging to ranchers and to the missions. Investigation led to the decision the ranch was too far off the beaten trail for a military installation.

In the spring of 1866 a band of twenty-six Paiute Indians camped beside the Mojave River at what is now the Victorville Narrows. A breathless runner came to them to tell of the white men operating sawmills on the mountain slopes, and ruining their happy-hunting-grounds in Little Bear Valley. The Indians went on the warpath

THE FIRST SAWMILL IN THE SAN BERNARDINO MOUNTAINS

It was owned by David and Wellington Seely, and stood at the lower end of Seely Flat. Water from a nearby creek furnished power for the mill to begin its work in 1853. The mill played a part in the Indian troubles ten years later. Lumber from this mill was used in building homes in San Bernardino.

immediately, their bodies streaked with war paint. Leaving their squaws and papooses sheltered in the Narrows, the Indians went up the river until they came to the Las Flores Ranch. Everyone was gone from the ranch except three young men — Ed Parish, Nefi Bemis, and Pratt Whitesides. The Indians, furious at the white men for invading their lands, killed and mutilated the three youths. Feeling revenge had been satisfied for the time, the Indians went back to the Narrows, and their families came out of hiding.

A year or so later, finding they had not discouraged the white men by their raid on the ranch, and that the sawmills were still operating, and their enemies were building homes, they again went on the warpath. This time the Indians moved their families to a spring back of Chimney Rock, a natural monument at the north end of Lucerne Valley.

The Indians' pent-up wrath was first spent on burning the sawmill at Blue Jay which was owned by Frank L. Talmage, an 1862 settler. A battle followed in which several Indians were killed. They had dragged their dead and wounded along with them, hiding them in the tall mesquite. One white man was wounded in the leg, another in the shoulder. The Indian chief was killed by Talmage.

Accompanied by another settler, Talmage rode horseback to San Bernardino to organize a posse. About forty men, all expert trackers and hunters, joined the posse to trail the Indians. They could see by the indentations of the terrain that the Indians were dragging their wounded and dead along with them.

The Indians were not robbers; they were interested

only in driving the white people out of their hunting territory. They did not like the whirring sound of the sawmills, nor the logging operations that were ruining the land of their ancestors. The white men were determined that justice must be meted out to the Indians.

The trail led the pursuers thirty-five miles through the pine country and down the boulder-strewn slopes to Lucerne Dry Lake. For five miles across the sun-baked playa, they rode to Chimney Rock where the Indians had hidden their squaws and children. With the ensuing battle the Indian raids were over.

Las Flores has had several names. The one it now bears was given because of the abundance of wild flowers in the region. The Spanish version of the name has added romance to the fertile and pleasant country. Before the Civil War the ranch was called Dunlap for the owner, Frank Dunlap.

In 1860 James F. Houghton and Amos P. Houlton acquired the property by patents from the federal government; land laws were very liberal at that time. John Burcham, who also gave his name to the ranch, was a friend of Houghton's and became ranch manager and partner in the enterprise. His two sons, Charles A. and Albert A., assisted in the management. Burcham died in 1890 and his oldest son carried on the ranch operations with the help of his brother. Charles Burcham was married to a lady physician who later grubstaked him for two years of prospecting, and he became one of the three discoverers of the Yellow Aster Mine at Randsburg in 1895.

Among the many owners of the Las Flores Ranch were Victor C. Smith and Robert Garner. Garner sold

the holdings in 1931 to the Talmadge brothers, cattle-
men of Victor Valley. Almost a dozen names are entered in the list of owners of the ranch. The Talmages
sold the ranch in 1931 to the Carver Investment Company, which is still the owner.

The new owners added several thousand acres to the
ranch. The Carver Investment Company was composed
of two brothers and two sisters, residing in Southern
California. They maintained a well-operated ranch
which had the advantage of three separate and distinct
types of native forage ranges immediately adjacent to
each other so the cattle did not have to be moved long
distances between seasonal ranging.

A high line ditch was constructed on the ranch in
the early 1880s for irrigation. For years alfalfa was
raised on Las Flores as an aid in feeding the vast herds
of cattle. The stock thrived on the natural browse of
the fertile valley and raising of alfalfa was discontinued.[1]

The grazing area of the ranch went up into the mountain slopes for a number of years. This upper area was
once used as a quail sanctuary, operated by the State
Fish and Game Division. It was one of the three or
four largest refuges in the country for fowl.

Today the famous old ranch, situated in Summit Valley, still holds charm for those who seek the outdoors
for adventure and recreation with the hint of the old
West, and yet is as modern as the airstrip on the holdings.
Its ten thousand acres of fertile valley land, rolling hills,
mountain slopes, and winding streams, have kept step
with the changing trends of western life. While most of

[1] Carver Investment Co., "Report: Resources and Development of Las
Flores Ranch."

the buildings and fences are original, there are later additions to fit into the current needs for operation.

In March 1967, a hunting preserve was established on a part of the Las Flores holdings. The ranch has always been a cattle ranch — and it is today — but the number of the browsing cattle is fewer than in past decades, when government land was leased far up in the mountains. The Las Flores Hunting Preserve has been planned for the discriminating bird hunters.[2] The preserve is organized on a membership basis.

The hunting season is from September 15 through March 20. Wild fowl in the preserve include pheasant, chuker, quail, dove, and ducks; deer hunting is permitted. The birds are happy in the seclusion of their habitat — the green meadows, creek beds, trees, thickets, and ponds. The lakes and ponds are stocked with fish. Riding and round-up horses are a part of the Las Flores picture. The area is a natural place for photographers, artists, and meditating writers.

With the coming of dams and reservoirs, being constructed to store water and to hold back ravaging floods, there will be many changes in the beautiful land of Las Flores. The contour of the land — those mountains that once protected horse thieves and gave pasture to stolen stock — will be but a mention in a history book. Mountains will be cut away to make new roads, and other alterations will follow the pattern of the changing West.

---

[2] Ruth Rutledge, "A New Look at an Old Ranch," news feature in *Valley Report*, March 16, 1967.

THE MOJAVE RIVER AT MODERN VICTORVILLE

In the foreground are the new freeway bridge and the old "Rainbow" bridge both at the downstream end of the Upper Narrows

12

Green Pastures of Victor Valley

By the high road, by the low road,
And along the winding trail,
They came in high adventure
With a faith that could not fail.

Louisa Springer Ames,
from "Pioneers" in *Desert Magazine*

Victor Valley is one of the fifty valleys, small and large, that make up the Mojave Desert with its mountains, ravines, hills, gulches and salt flats. Victor Valley unofficially takes in Hesperia, even though this town is built upon mesa land. Apple Valley, also known as the East Mesa, lies east of the river. The larger area, lying west of the river, comes naturally into the designation of West Mesa.

West Mesa includes an area of eight to ten miles to the west of Victorville that, some thirty years ago, was called Sunrise Valley, reaching in the general direction of the El Mirage country where today there is a soaring field. The elevated portions of this area, to the southwest where the Phelan post office is located, is called Baldy Mesa.

Included in this unofficial arrangement of valleys, is Adelanto. Adjacent to Adelanto is the George Air Force Base which has been a training station for a number of years. It was established prior to World War II.

Lucerne Valley, which claims a town and a dry lake, is about fifteen miles from the Mojave River, and is on the old Holcomb Trail; it seems to fit itself into the life of Victor Valley both socially and politically.

Victorville is the largest town in the Upper Mojave Valley. It has advanced far beyond its status of a half century ago. It is now progressing consistently with the trend of modern living. The river forms its northern and eastern boundaries.

Hesperia was on the line of travel in the very early days of the white man's westward migration. The earliest date recorded on the Hesperia settlement is 1869.[1]

An interesting story is told by Dr. Edmund C. Jaeger, an eminent scientist. In the spring of 1918, Dr. Jaeger made a trip to California's Palomar Mountains for a period of rest and relaxation. In a far-back country region he came upon an abandoned building that was only seven by nine feet in size. The small cabin with a lean-to that evidently had served as a post-office, was named "Nellie" for the daughter of a man named McQueen who had been the postmaster. The house was open to the elements, and weeds and brushes were growing through the pane-less windows and the door-less doors. It was one of San Diego County's earliest post offices.

The walls inside the main building had been papered with layers of news sheets from old *San Diego Union* newspapers which bore dates between 1882 and 1889. Where they were hanging loose and dangling to the floor, mice were nibbling at the tasty dried wheat-flour paste.

---

[1] Edmund C. Jaeger, "The Ghost That Refuses to Die," in *Desert Magazine*, August 1954.

Dr. Jaeger tore off the sheets and began idly to read the still legible print. One paper told of "Hesperia on the Mojave River, Denver of the West." The projected city's promoters indidicated it was destined to have a glorious future. There would be several hundred thousand population. Hundreds of acres would be planted to fruit — peaches, apricots, vineyards. Three parks were on the blueprint with a new hotel to be built of bricks made on the spot. There would be a newspaper, to be called the "Hesperia Herald," which would be the largest in the county. The Atlantic and Pacific Railroad would run through the heart of the town.

A few years later, the scientist visited Hesperia. He found it a far cry from the news article in the mice-nibbled old San Diego newspapers. There was only a large hotel, a single store, a small railway station, a red brick schoolhouse, and six or seven houses — all in disrepair. Two women were operating the hotel.

Dr. Jaeger was thoroughly intrigued with the mesa country's history and later made a trip to the San Bernardino archives to poke around in old property records. He found that on July 10, 1869, Max Strobel acquired thirty-five thousand acres in the Upper Mojave River region. He paid forty-four thousand dollars for the land from the United States government Land Office. He turned the land over to a group of Germans on August 2, 1871, who proposed to sub-divide and colonize the property.

The next year this same parcel of land was acquired by the Thirty-fifth Parallel Association, a San Francisco land company. This was the same group of German associates reorganized under a new name, and their

NOTICE OF APPROPRIATION OF WATER.

In San Bernardino ~~County~~ California

The undersigned desiring to appropriate the water hereinafter refered to, pursuant to the laws of the State of California, hereby give notice, by posting this notice this 15th day of March 1886 in a conspicuous place at the point of intended diversion, stating herein:

1st. That the undersigned claims the water there flowing in the East Fork of the Mojave River Cal. *to the extent of* five thousand *inches measured under a four inch pressure.*

2d. The water is claimed for the purpose of using the same for irrigating and for domestic purposes, and for water power. The place of intended use is upon the lands of The Hesperia Land & Water Company in Townships 3. 4. & 5. N. Range 4 W. S.B.M. Called Hesperia

3d. The means by which the undersigned intend to divert said water, are A dam at the point of diversion, which is in Sec. 15. T.3N. R. 3 W. S.B.M. at which point a monument of ten large stones is placed on the southerly bank of said river from which place the water will be conducted in ditches flumes and pipes of sufficient capacity to conduct said 5000 inches of water onto said lands.

Dated and posted in a conspicuous place at the point of intended diversion the 15 th day of March 1886.

The Hesperia Land & Water Co.
By R. M. Widney President
" H. L. McNeil Secretary

Recorded at request of
Wells Fargo & Co
March 25 th A.D. 1886
at 11 A. M. in Book B of
Water Records p. 302
Sequar Allen
County Recorder.

HESPERIA'S WATER CLAIM OF 1886

Almost a century ago, residents were concerned about securing water for the townsite that was being laid out for settlement. A ditch was dug and lined with concrete to bring the water from Deep Creek. The company's land was Hesperia's first purchased federal land — bought through land agent Max Strobel.

Courtesy of Florence Edgington Elwell.

plan failed to materialize in any way. On April 10, 1885, the association sold to Julius Finck who, six days later, sold to a man named McNeil. The following year, on May 6, McNeil sold to the Hesperia Land and Water Company. This firm was made up of the same group of people that had laid out the town of Ontario, California. And thereby hangs a tale.

In every deed to the lots sold there was a stipulation that if liquor was ever "sold, served or given away," even if in the center of the streets facing the property, the land would revert to the company immediately.

The arrangements that were laid out for the town were pleasing in patterns, size and price. Water had already been brought down from Deep Creek through a concrete-lined ditch into a siphon and pipe line, which carried water to a reservoir in Hesperia.

After a great deal of land was sold (even as far away as England) a new land company was formed to keep the boom alive. A Los Angeles newspaper reported in October 1887,

> One of the most important purchases of real estate ever recorded in Southern California was made yesterday afternoon by the following capitalists from New York: Lieutenant C. A. Barnes, S. A. Fleming and C. A. Smith, in connection with eminent capitalists from other parts of the country.

The sale took in the waters of the East Fork (Deep Creek) of the Mojave, the ditch and pipe line and the townsite of Hesperia. Grandiose plans were perfected. A big hotel and a sanitarium, with price figures in seven digits, were considered.

Fifteen miles of sidewalks and a half-dozen reservoirs were to be constructed. A well-secured bank; two million

HESPERIA'S FIRST SCHOOL HOUSE, ERECTED IN 1891

THE HESPERIA HOTEL, ERECTED IN 1890

It boasted thirteen rooms and a bath on each of the upper floors, with electric call bells, speaking tubes to the office, indoor plumbing and hot water. On the ground floor was a lobby, dining room, kitchen, office, and store

dollars assured for city improvements; a railroad running through the tract; and water, water, everywhere, were promised. They would irrigate with the percolating system that had been so successfully used in Fresno County. They would raise deciduous fruits and the vineyards would lead to the manufacture of raisins. The fruit-planting would be on the largest scale ever begun in the world.

Hesperia was all set again with rosy promises and was ready to work for and reap a harvest. Maybe it might have happened that way if things had continued to go along as planned. Though the area was off to a good start, two successive years of bad Mojave floods washed out the aqueduct line that was the life-artery of the region. Before it could be repaired properly and permanently, the young orchards died and the little vines withered. People left for other fields of endeavor. Hesperia, which had been named for its Greek meaning of western lands, went back to the desert and the solitude of her imploring Joshua trees. The big hotel was boarded up with its past and left with its grand stairway, its fireplaces and its modern speaking-tube system, and its dreams of grandeur. "Denver of the West" wafted from the dreams as did the strains of the beautiful music from Paderewski's artistic fingers as he had whiled away some of his time at the hotel while waiting for a train connection.

Hesperia was to have yet another chance; so her dreams were dreamed again. While it did not turn out to be the "Denver of the West," it came within her own environs as Hesperia-on-the-Mesa.

The early siphon that carried water to Hesperia was

in use until the mid-'forties when it was no longer needed. The siphon is gone forever, but sections of the pipe line that first brought water to Hesperia, can now be found underground when excavations are made. The original fourteen-inch piping was changed to thirty-inch in the interim of the years to expedite the flow of water through the seven-mile distance to the first reservoir. The reservoir was filled in when the Hesperia Community Center was built over it.

From the time the railroad entered the Hesperia area there were always a few people there trying to make a living or enjoying retirement. At one time potatoes were raised in the area in large quantities, and the old hotel gave its last bit of usefulness serving as a storehouse for the earthy vegetable. The hotel was torn down during the early 'sixties. It had become unsafe.

The town was thoroughly rehabilitated, starting in 1954, under still another real estate venture. This one brought stability to the little town on the mesa. The residents have a great love for their Joshua trees; as far as they are concerned the Joshuas are there to stay — and there are many of them.

This great venture for the little "western-land" town was managed under the name of Hesperia Land and Development Company, owned and operated by M. Penn Phillips, one of the nation's largest real estate developers. This was considered as the second largest land sale in California. The community that refused so many times to become a ghost town and steadfastly followed its lodestar, is now a respected town in many aspects. Beginning with an interest in obtaining week-end property for pleasure and speculation, it has grown to a population of about eight thousand. These persons are content to go on living there and building their town around the "western flavor." Built on the mesa, the air is bracing, and the views are extravaganzas. Every type of business is operating in Hesperia. The holdings of the famous Hesperia Inn have been purchased for a military school for boys. The Joshua trees give the area an exotic atmosphere with their contorted limbs forming odd shapes, and the white, waxy blossoms appearing foreign to the trees' odd shapes.[2]

The Mojave, with its strange ebb and flow, rolls through the hill country below the mountain slopes after it becomes one river and starts its hide-and-seek existence through the broad sandy channel. When the river leaves the mesa, it runs under a wide bridge that marks an accepted boundary between Hesperia and Apple Valley. The bridge is long enough and wide enough, to take care of ordinary floods, but now and then the waters go on a rampage as any surface river might do. Almost any day water can be seen glaring at the onlooker, apparently in a still, submissive state; but it will be moving in its own unorthodox way, beneath its deposited sand.

Apple Valley is one of Victor Valley's components. It is shaped like a large bowl. Mountains on every horizon-curve surround it and there is a fine view in all directions except in times when the winds are gnashing and the earth's smallest particles are lifted, obstructing the sight of the hills and mountains with yellow curtains. When one adult was bemoaning the fact that "my moun-

---
[2] Its true name is *yucca brevifolia*; it belongs to the lily family.

tains are gone," a little four-year-old boy replied, "Never mind, they are just covered up with dirt."

Apple Valley is partly a "planned town," so population is kept under control and industry has yet to come into the desert resort community. Not all the development companies make rigid rules, and in time it may outgrow itself. Now and then a sub-division rises and new streets are created. The early Indians called the valley "Happy Valley" and legend says even warlike Indians were peaceful when in the Apple Valley bowl. Almost all of the streets have Indian names.

It was in 1910 when Apple Valley really began to emerge as an entity. Homesteaders were coming in large numbers. There had been a school for almost a decade, located at the intersection of Bear Valley and Deep Creek roads.

In February 1946, the first real efforts to make a settled region of the big desert bowl occurred when Newton Bass (reputedly a multi-millionaire from oil-field revenue) came to the region with the avowed purpose of raising cattle. The cattle plans gave way, and real estate development and sales took over.

The heart of Apple Valley is the village site where all types of business, required to meet the daily needs of life, line the two access roads on either side of Highway 18 — service stations, grocers, drugs, cleaners, mercantile branches, and banks. It has its schools; and more people keep coming. There is a gradual boom in the air. Some day Apple Valley will catch up with its boundaries and become a city. The valley and the town are really one.

Apple Valley, Victorville, and Hesperia form a tri-city.

They inter-lock with fraternal groups, veteran groups, churches, social life — yet each community wants to be set apart. Each area has its own chamber of commerce, its community buildings, its special days. Each has an annual day to show its individuality. Yet each combine in the attempt to bring the past back to the present. Victorville has its "Stellabration," Hesperia its "Hesperia Days," and Apple Valley its "Pow Wow." There are parades with all the trappings — with riders and mounts, floats and bands. There is an annual queen for each area.

However, there is a lot of stepping over the invisible line of demarcation and the three communities may easily be construed as one. There is a great feeling for early settler communication. An active group of people, with a dedicated feeling for preserving old memories, land-marks, early-day families and history, has formed an historical society to weld together the old with the new.

Its appellation is one of the great mysteries of Apple Valley. Most of the populace would like to say that the area was named Apple Valley because it raised so many apples. They always recall that just as many peaches, pears, apricots and cherries were raised by the early settlers. So head-scratching starts when the subject arises. Some would like to say that it was named for a man called Appleton, probably the one who was a member of a water company, or as one legend says, was sent out by the government to control the hostile Indians. They can't even find out who named it. The historical society of the region takes the mystery seriously and is busy tracing records and running down clues, but it is always just short on proof.

About the only site of historic significance in the area

(except the Mojave River) is Deadman's Point, which is at the intersection of Highway 18 and Bear Valley Road. It was on the line of the Van Dusen Road that was built by miners of the gold camp at Holcomb Valley in the 1860s.

A cluster of magnificent rocks is formed on a slightly sloping area, fantastically shaped and eerie-looking. A forty-acre surface spreading out from the base of the rocks glares in the summer sun with compelling heat. The rocks proved a shelter for pioneer traffic, for shade and rest, and from rain and snow and blowing, biting sand.

Its caves and coves were good camping and hiding places. The clustered pile forms a backdrop for the intentionally drab buildings of the small "western village" that represents recreation for the people of the tri-city desert area. It is suggestive of the nineteenth century with its false front buildings, western band, hitching rail, red-checked tablecloths and curtains; it has a "Long Branch-Gunsmoke" flavor. Some of the early Victor Valley residents say that Lucky Baldwin came down from his mountain mines to Deadman's Point to gamble — the gambling room being a cave back in the granite rocks. The Point opens up controversial subjects, chief of which is how it got its name. That remains a choice mystery in the region with no proof of any version.

Victorville has long been the hub of development in Victor Valley, from the time people began coming through the Mojave Desert. It is fortunately situated where there is water the year around. The lands along the river bottom are attractive even as in early settlement years. A river, even of the Mojave type, has many potentials for a new country.

The first occupants of the fertile lands of the valley, in 1860 near the Upper Narrows, were two men named Bemis and Hancock. They did not stay long as the hostile Indians ran them off. Historical works often refer to the two men as "taking up homesteads." However, prior to 1862 there were no homestead laws for acquiring property on the desert — if one wanted a piece of land, he simply appropriated it and lived upon it. In many instances land was pre-empted. Relinquishments were available also under the unwritten and liberal land laws of the time. This was probably how the two men, Bemis and Hancock acquired their land.

Later history finds the name of Bemis in the river valley. One man named Bemis possessed the "Mohave Ranch," which was located near Helendale. L. Burr Belden, desert historian, tells of a Mrs. Jerusha Bemis who brought her children across the desert, her husband having died enroute to the West. There is an annual family reunion held in the county for the Bemis-Hancock-Roberds clan. Detailed history is not available but it is quite likely that these may be descendants of the two who settled on the land that is the famous Verde Ranch (now the Kemper Campbell Ranch).

Over on the Summit Valley lands there was activity in 1860. The first settlement there was by means of the liberal approach to land law. In the Oro Grande section, A. G. Lane became owner of land along the river which was known as Lane's Crossing. He was still operating his "homestead" in 1868, having come to the area in 1861.

A very modern concrete bridge spans the Upper Narrows and carries Highway 18 across into Victorville from Apple Valley. After reaching the Victorville side of the river, a street turns to the left and leads to the present Campbell Ranch. There have been a number of bridges through the years over this narrow gorge. The new bridge's predecessor, still standing, is owned and used by a cement firm. It is so small that it is dwarfed by the new bridge.

Rumor has run strong through the decades about the first occupant of the famed ranch which had been called the Brown Ranch and the Verde before it received the current name. Homestead records have not come up with any answer, and it has clung to the Brown usage rather consistently.

John Brown, Sr., who was very busy helping the West to grow, receives some of the honor for the name, although there is no proof that he lived on the Narrows ranch lands. Brown had a large family, consisting of four boys and six girls. Three of the boys — John, Joseph, and James — have had property in their names. Little is said of the other son, Newton.

There has been a strong feeling that John Brown, Jr., may well have been the one who lived there and for whom the ranch was named. There is a document that may settle the question:

RANCHO VERDE COMPANY

Rancho Verde includes 3,800 acres in the Mojave River bottom just above the Upper Narrows. The first occupation was about 1867 by James Brown, a cattleman who pre-empted land and by 1874 had 1,500 acres fenced and a ditch from the river. Cole and Harris, who acquired the property about 1894, added more land by purchase, constructed another ditch, drilled wells and started a dairy.[3]

In 1870 James Brown built a house that was called "The Red House" and which is still standing and in use as a residence, ninety-nine years later. There are a couple of other buildings on the ranch that are equally as old and are used for storage. The house can be seen from the road.

There have been many changes in the ranch's ownership which research will bring to light some day. It is not known who gave it the name of Verde, though it is a very appropriate name. In spring the site is lovely with old, sturdy, heavily-branched trees and myriads of early flowers.

From its beginning, the Verde was a working ranch, and remains so under its latest ownership. The ranch was purchased in 1924 by Mr. and Mrs. Kemper Campbell. They had a partner named Sorenson. At that time the size of the ranch was four thousand acres. Sometime through the passing years the ranch was divided, creating the North Verde and the South Verde. The Campbells, a husband and wife team of lawyers in Los Angeles, acquired the ranch for week-end recreation, but it has also remained a working ranch. When the Campbells retired they made their home at the Verde.

The following, by an unknown writer, is said to have been dedicated to the famed Verde:

> The house is yours;
> Its portals open wide, and welcome you to all inside.
> Friend and guest, enter in peace, and rest;
> The house is yours.

---

[3] W. F. McClure (State Engineer), and others, *Mojave River Commission: Report on the Utilization of Mojave River for Irrigation in Victor Valley, California* (State of Calif., Dept. of Engineering, Bulletin no. 5), p. 23.

Many famous persons made the old ranch a haven for rest and found it a good place for continuing their writing, painting, music, and other creative arts.

J. B. Priestly, who wrote *Midnight on the Desert*, told about the old ranch in his book. He had fallen for the desert's fascination. He loved the plant life and the colors of the sky in both evening and morning. He described the big sitting-room with its wooden galleries and rafters and the enormous open brick fireplace that he had enjoyed while living there as a guest. He told of the picnic suppers they had outside and how they enjoyed the western evenings.

Some unknown aficionado who was fascinated by the desert and felt its spell, found many colorful things about the desert that seemed dull and drab to the majority of people who came and went in those days when the desert's charm had not become so universal. This unknown person found the desert green where water "stirred its fertile soil." He noticed gray and lavender on the mesas instead of desolation. He wrote of the "blue and gray of new desert" and the "geranium" of young shrubs. He found pink and purple in the mountains. "Here the tender twilight or the fresh dawn of the desert may be enjoyed in the shade of the terrace or beside a quiet lake."

Before the railroad came through the Victor Valley region, the stage stops were called by the name of whatever person owned or operated the line or station. Perhaps the last individual to be in charge was John C. Turner, a pioneer of the valley. The Turners had located on a fine agricultural site about half way between today's Victorville and Oro Grande. The Turners operated a hotel for lodging and eating as well as a stage stop.

Later, John Turner opened up the first place of business in Victorville, a general store.

Long years before there were any transcontinental facilities such as stages and trains, the settlement at the river crossing was called Mormon Crossing. This name carried on for about seven years. The Mormons did not fully follow the trails of the earlier explorers and pathfinders. The majority of the Mormon travelers were coming west for home-building so they cruised about the canyons and passes for spots where they could take their wagons through the mountains, or at least where it was feasible to dismantle them and get them over, then reassemble them. They were pretty well loaded with home furnishings and there were bitter experiences when many precious belongings had to be abandoned to facilitate travel.

There is a story of a certain contingent of Mormons who were camped near the Crossing, ready to take off for a pass the following morning. During the night, to their utter dismay, they were awakened by a roaring, thundering noise. It was the Mojave in a rampage of flood waters. They climbed to higher ground and there they remained for three weeks. One man insisted on trying to get through and was drowned. It was during the yule holiday time and they had hoped to get through to join others of the Mormon cavalcade.

Mormon Crossing was given the name of Huntington when the railroad came through the area. The name was again changed to honor Jacob N. Victor, construction superintendent during the building of the rail lines through the desert and Cajon regions. Complications arose as the Santa Fe had a town on its line in Colorado named Victor. The desert town was then changed to Victorville. However, Victor Valley still carries his name. John Brown's toll road added much to the advancement of the desert valley. The road was completed in June 1861. This active and enterprising pioneer of San Bernardino County built the twelve-mile road to facilitate travel into and out of the desert over the Cajon route. This road became one of the vital links with the East and, according to latter day historians, much of it has been paralleled by present-day travel routes.[4]

Brown secured a franchise for building and maintaining the road. He was assisted in the project by Henry M. Willis, then district attorney of San Bernardino, and George L. Tucker, also of San Bernardino County. The franchise was to run for twenty years, after which time the road would be taken over for public use. It was to connect with the Van Dusen Road from Holcomb Valley to the desert floor. At the end of eighteen years, the road was leased to other parties for the balance of the franchise term. Two toll-road gates were operated. It is interesting to note in the Beattie book that the travel from Los Angeles and San Bernardino went into Bill Holcomb's delightful valley over the "Brown Turnpike." The newspapers described the toll road as "The Old Spanish Trail made into a good road having grass and water within easy distance."[5]

From time to time through the years, Victorville has been of interest to the motion picture companies, particularly for western films. The false fronts, narrow

---

[4] Sylvester, *Mohahve* (1964).
[5] Beattie, *Heritage of the Valley* (1939), p. 337.

streets, the old corrals, and the wildness of the river's Upper Narrows, were desirable features for location sites.

For many years rodeos were a great part of Victorville's recreation and entertainment, and horses are important in today's recreation for the tri-cities of Victor Valley. New streets are being laid out, housing projects are modern in style, and the present era is making the town a fair-sized little city with many new business projects.

There seems to be a modern trend in "booming" in the area. Freeways have made it less like a far-away region of desertland. Men and machinery are changing the mountain and desert areas with dams and reservoirs. The underground river which for months at a time flows along slowly and unseen, still breaks out in raging floods and torrents, changing the desert floor into gullies and ravines, washing away bridges and ruining streets. In flood the stream is like any ordinary surface river, and proves its ancient heritage as a mighty river. Flood control agencies are making strides these days to change all that.

This "percolating" stream (as engineers and geologists describe a river of the Mojave's type) is sometimes a fickle waterway, changing its habits, forming new and old channels, and swampy areas.

13

The Story of Oro Grande

So let me live where I can hear
The silken whisper of the sand,
The singing music of the sphere,
The light-wing feet, the unseen hand
Of pressing winds that murmur near
The pulsing spirit of the land.

Paul Wilhelm,
from *Desert Magazine,* May 1954

A trading post was an open door to friendliness in a pioneer desert land. Its very make-up was a beckoning welcome for those who came near. A passer-by saw a light and traveled toward it. He knew there would be some sort of civilization behind that door. A trading post was for the man who smoked, the one who chewed, and the one who tipped his elbow. The work shirt needed buttons; there would be the inevitable sewing kit holding needles and thread. There would be a piece of cloth for the doll's bonnet and a stick of horehound candy for an ailing child. There he would find a deck of cards for the lonely desert night and oil for the lamps of a desert shack. There would be companionship for a time, a chance to talk about the flood last week, the cow that mired in the swamp, and fearsome lurking Indians. The choking, bitter thoughts of a homesick heart would be eased for a little while.

A river bend was a good place for a trading post.

The Mojave was quite a respectable stream at the point that was only a crossing in the 'fifties and 'sixties of a century ago. Its bends swept the waters in a pleasant way; the grass grew tall, and the cottonwoods whispered of the life that was past, and the new one that was forming along the ancient river bed.

Before there was a town just across the river from the post, this point was an oasis. It had been settled in 1861 by A. G. Lane, who built a fort-like cabin with a port-hole from which he could peer out to watch for, and shoot at, Indians. The walls were double, built of the abundant cottonwoods that gave the spot its cozy look. It was called Lane's Crossing in the early years of desert travel. The river could be crossed by wagons and horses and a foot-bridge led across from bank to bank. It was only a few miles from the Turner ranch and stage stop, and near the Lower Narrows where today a large bridge spans the gap.

Seven years after he homesteaded his land, Lane wrote the following letter to the San Bernardino *Guardian*:

> My station is immediately on the river—seven miles from the upper crossing. The land on the Mojave, the point where I am, is exceedingly fertile and comparatively free from alkali.
>
> It is of that peculiar character which retains moisture well and consequently I am able to cultivate successfully without irrigation. I irrigated my garden this season, but planted in the proper time it would not have been necessary to do so. On the 160 acres of land which I have taken as a home-stead, there are 100 acres of land well adapted to farming purposes. My place is well timbered and I have as good water as there is in the world.
>
> I command grazing land sufficient for several head of

THE LOWER NARROWS AND BRIDGE, THREE MILES NORTH OF VICTORVILLE

Both the Lower and Upper Narrows share the same geologic history, and both
served for many years as a recreation and picnic area

stock. You can judge of the quality of grass when I tell you . . . I am supplying Camp Cady . . . with beef and the soldiers swear it is the best they ever ate.

In conclusion, Messers. Editors, allow me to give you an invitation to come and see me. I can feast you upon wild game and fish as well as green corn and all root vegetables, etc.

A. G. LANE

Pioneer records of the Oro Grande country (which included Lane's Crossing) are sketchy, but through the years since the first settlements, there are some facts that have been garnered for history. Lane's settlement led the way, and eventually other homesteads were taken as the area expanded across the river.

Gold was found near here in 1868. The first mine is said to have been either discovered by E. L. Doheny, or he purchased it, and gave it the name of Oro Grande meaning "Big Gold." The name was also given to the village that was established later. When the railroad came through in the 'eighties, the name of Halleck was given to the town. (There are conflicting reasons for the name of Halleck: one is that it was the name of an official in the cement industry that was established there; the other that it was for a man active in the California state legislature.) According to R. V. "Penny" Morrow, eighty-two-year-old resident of Oro Grande, the citizens got together and successfully petitioned to have the name of Oro Grande restored to the town.

The early settlers found it a good country. Cattle ranged far back into the hills, but always returned to the water that was then continuous on the surface of the river bed at that point. Wild game was plentiful in those early years and included wild boar, lynx and deer. Wild bird life abounded.

A stamp mill was constructed when gold was discovered. The site of the Oro Grande Mining and Milling Company was only a few miles from the town. It was closed about the time of World War II. Another mine of some importance was the Carbonate Mine, which also closed about the same time. During the silver boom in Calico, ore was hauled eighty miles over the rough desert roads to Oro Grande for milling. Later, the Calico mining interests purchased the mill and hauled it to the Calico mines.

The Carbonate Mine was important because its slanting main shaft struck a rich limestone deposit. The mine was worked by another company and the Carbonate was pushed out of business with a good supply of gold still available. One man, T. J. Fleming, made some improvements in burning methods, and later became the founder of the California Portland Cement Company at Colton.[1]

Oro Grande suffered as a town in these later years when the freeway by-passed it, but fortunately the cement industry keeps it alive. Today, alfalfa fields follow the river, pumping plants hum, and the cottonwoods still make a pleasing line along the old river bed.

In 1907 a woman was active in starting the cement plant at Oro Grande. She was Mrs. E. M. Potts who came from England to Southern California as a bride in the middle 'eighties. Visioning the future, this dynamic woman of industry was joined in her venture by girlhood friends. Most of the capital was English money.

---

[1] L. Burr Belden, in San Bernardino *Sun-Telegram*, Aug. 28, 1955.

Her spirit for the work was infectious and her friends rallied around her whenever there were financial problems. She always stuck to her post with the tenacity of the English. Convincing men with money to invest in a desert enterprise was not always an easy thing to swing, but for many years she was successful in her efforts.

Mr. Potts was a well-known architect and toured the country inspecting cement mills for ideas for the desert industry. He spent five years with the Oro Grande cement firm, helping with the building of the plant and aiding the operation. He died about 1911 or 1912. Both he and his wife were well liked and respected.

It is recalled by old timers of the community that when "Madame," as she was called good-naturedly, was going to arrive every worker turned out to get the plant in the best of shape — not from any fear of rebuke, but because of their genuine liking for her.

There are few old timers left in Oro Grande. A dozen years ago they sat on benches in the sun and shade and dreamed of the days gone by. Eyes, trained to see long distances, were steel-like and needed only one quick look to judge those who came to sit on the benches with them. If the visitor had a genuine desire to know of their past days he was welcomed by the miners and prospectors, and could sit companionably with them on the benches. They would walk to the high hill above the town and help an interested one search for Oro Grande's own type of tree rock, which is now practically extinct. The tree rock was not fossilized; it was formed by chemical action. From that hilltop a splendid panorama spreads out over the desert valley, the river well-marked by trees.

Raymond Victor Morrow, known far and wide for

many years as "Penny," has well earned the title of "Father of Oro Grande." He came to the area when he was an infant. He is still a citizen of Oro Grande, spending only about five years away from the desert in his four-score years. Very little has happened constructively in his town in which he has not had a hand. He came from pioneer stock. His grandfather Morrow made two trips driving cattle from Missouri to Stockton, California. He was one of the early legislators of the state of California.

Penny is the only remaining member of his family. He had one sister, and three brothers — Roy, Jim and Harry. None of the brothers married. They spent their years actively in mining, farming, and business. The two older brothers, Roy and Jim, discovered a turquoise mine in the Slocum Mountains in 1898 and worked it for many years. The other brothers helped now and then, but usually were interested in other matters. Their father, Newton L. Morrow, came to the desert in 1857, and was an early judge and recorder in San Bernardino County.

Turquoise somehow never seemed to reach valuable status while the Morrow "boys" were busy mining it, and they turned their attention mostly to copper mining. By the time turquoise was of interest in value, the brothers had lost the mine. It disappeared, and they never relocated it. Such things as cloud-bursts on the desert can wipe out a location completely. The mine is probably now enclosed within the boundaries of the United States Navy property and thus is inaccessible.

Penny went away to school in his younger years and meant to establish himself in Southern California. But he heard from Mrs. Potts that a barber was badly needed for the two to three hundred men in Oro Grande, so Penny packed up his barber tools and went "home" to stay — and is still there. However, the barber trade was only a part of the many activities with which Penny was concerned. He became a merchant, postmaster, constable, grange master, an agricultural inspector, school trustee, road commissioner, and member of the water district of San Bernardino County.

Oro Grande had its own celebrity, too — one of Penny Morrow's contemporaries. He was "Buster" (Thomas Richard) Bennington, said to be the last of the famous mule-team drivers. He was a schoolmate of Penny's, and for many years they were neighbors. Bennington was called a "long jerk-liner." He explained that by telling how he learned the trade of driving ten- and sixteen-mule teams for the limestone industry northeast of Oro Grande. This thriving industry today is owned by Riverside Cement Company.

The famous driver told how the limerock was loaded into the mule-drawn wagons by way of chutes. The thirty-six-pound rocks were lifted and reloaded by hand labor into freight gondolas on railroad spurs about four miles from the mine. (Sugar refineries needed the lime in its pure state for processing their products.)

Two lead mares were driven and guided by a single rope. Two jerks on the line told the leaders a right turn would be made. A single jerk meant a left turn. "They were plumb smart," Buster Bennington said. "They knowed a straight pull over every time meant left! Especially when the barns were close."

In the 1890s Bennington worked for a firm named

Mahoney Brothers. He drove a "cracking good" sixteen-mule team between Lancaster and Bakersfield. He could harness a mule a minute — a very fast record. Ten mules in ten minutes! In Penny Morrow's private museum of antiques and relics of the western desert there is a prized mule-team bell from Bennington's teams.

A few miles from Oro Grande, downstream on the Mojave River, the small town of Helendale is located. There is an attractive site with tall trees following the line of the river. In years past a great many cattle grazed over a vast range.

The people of Helendale are justly proud of their fine new school plant. This is the fourth schoolhouse to be built there. Another school building is still standing but not in school use.

The story is told of the new post office in Helendale. The old post-office building was not the newest or the most comfortable one in the area. It seems that one day in the post office a lady was startled by a snake, with its head lifted, gliding into the room. In less time than it takes to tell about it, she was standing in the rocking-chair yelling for help, which soon arrived. In record time, a new post-office building was constructed.

Helendale was originally called Point of Rocks. One record says the name was changed to Helen, the daughter of a railroad official. Later, the suffix "dale" was added to the name as fitting for the pastoral type of region that makes the area so pleasant.

Nine miles further downstream from Helendale is a railroad stop called Hodge. In the spring of 1913 two brothers, Gilbert and Robert Hodge, left their home in New York for a vacation in Southern California. While there they learned of the free government land on the Mojave Desert. They made a trip to the desert and it captured their fancy. They settled on homestead land and made plans to remain on it. They purchased a team of pintos and a second-hand wagon which they loaded with provisions and farming equipment, including a plow. They added water barrels, blankets, chickens, wire, a woodstove and staple foods. It was a difficult trip over the mountain roads, taking six days to get from Los Angeles to the summit of Cajon where they had a sublime view of the desert.

At the homestead, they built a corral for the ponies, enclosed their chickens from the hazards of coyotes, fastened their tent securely from the winds, and began to improve the land.

The nearest neighbor of the Hodge brothers was the eminent Arthur Brisbane, columnist and editor of a San Francisco newspaper. The brothers were often mentioned in his column and they visited in his Santa Barbara home. Brisbane had an office constructed on the railroad and added a telegraph set-up so that he could wire his column and news to the *Examiner* office in the bay city while he was at his ranch, which was quite frequently.

Although the Hodge brothers had homesteads near the river they were unable to find water on their land. After they received their patents in 1914, they set about to prove up on another claim. Obtaining this type of free land was different than by the regular Homestead Act. The government required one dollar to be spent per acre for five years including the sowing of permanent crops, developing water at two points, and other specified requirements.

The new claims were closer to the Mojave River and they felt sure they could reach water. They did at eighteen feet. The brothers made a complete and thorough study of alfalfa, planted it, and it became their "green gold," for they prospered and had nice homes in the community.

The settlements that were formed in the early days changed with the passing of the years. Each era brought something new and needful to the little towns along the river; each also took something away. Mining had its day. The gold went out of the picture, but the limestone took over, and proved as great a need. Agricultural pursuits developed and enriched the land, but it reduced the quantity of water in the river.

The railroads came and replaced the stages and stage stations. Wagon freighting gave way to the swiftness of the iron horse. The motor vehicles came and highways replaced the lanes and dirt roads. The freeways were built and towns were by-passed because distance had to be cut. Some communities and towns declined because of this by-passing. Others stood steadfast; still others went ahead, regardless.

Oro Grande is still a town. It has its cement industry which saved it from the graveyard of ghost towns. Helendale, though not on the freeway, still has its lushness and the serenity of a pastoral community. Time cannot be stopped; nor can progress and change be denied.

There is philosophy for towns as well as for people.

14

The Kingdom of the Sun

Give me the splendid silent sun,
with all its beams full blazing!
Walt Whitman

Back in the second decade of the twentieth century, a group of Mojave River Valley residents banded together to bring out a magazine for the pleasure of the desert people, for the purpose of bringing them cultural and social advantages, and blending them together in their common interest of life on the Mojave.

They called the periodical *Kingdom of the Sun.* Its coverage took in the twelve valleys adjacent to Victor Valley, including the areas of Oro Grande, Apple Valley, Hesperia, Victorville, and El Mirage Valley. While there was no absolute line of division, the land from Oro Grande to the Adelanto region was called Sunrise Valley. Victorville and Apple Valley stood on their own names, with Hesperia included as well in the over-all "Kingdom of the Sun."

The magazine, which was started in 1912, expected to have two issues a year. For some reason, the existing editions of the magazine do not carry a date line. There were not more than three of these issues that saw the light of publication. A great deal of thought and planning went into the little magazines which for the most part were quite scholarly, and bring to these later days the fact that during 1912 to 1914, the desert was being settled by people of education, and of well-rounded lives in their years before coming to the desert.

New homestead acts for reclaiming desert lands went into effect during these years and somehow in most of the stories of these later settlers there is missing the note of great hardships that came down with history of generations beyond the turn of the century. The majority of the new type of settler seemed to have come with plenty of financial planning for their homesteading.

The magazines appear somewhat quaint in comparison to the periodicals of today. However, in reading the issues one finds nothing outside the pale of good taste. The issues are, of course, out of print, and very few are known to exist now. It measures six inches wide by twice that in length. Attractive art and illustration, much of it of settlers and of people and their descendants indicates the feeling of family life. The photography, considering the state of its development to that time, is quite good. Much use was made of stories and poems. In fact, the payment for a year's subscription was one dollar plus several "gems of thoughts" from well-known and scholarly writings.

L. Dana was editor and publisher of the *Kingdom of the Sun*. Lillian D. Gregory was the business manager and A. C. Lester was Life-O-Graph editor. The photographic illustrations reflected the interests of the times — farming, recreation, education, social life, and all that goes to make up a community. The issues were also liberally sprinkled with art work.

The publication survived only a little less than two

years when it ceased and became part of the history of more than half a century ago.

Headquarters of the magazine was Oro Grande, which at one time boasted two thousand residents. The printing of the magazine was done in Los Angeles. The hundreds of pictures were finished in San Bernardino.

Throughout the little books (the issues were glued and stapled) the basis of presentation format was the "homestead." In two of the three issues there is a page which more or less fits the spot of a table of contents. "The Home 40" has listed below the title The Local, Hearthstone, Commercial and Campfire Sections with such topics added as follows: Where the Eagle Screams (county affairs): Binding Wire, Crate and Gunnysack Items; Shadowgraphs — Yesterday, Today and Tomorrow; The Hoot of the Desert Owl (people); Wise Sayings by Wise Men; The Kingdom's Guest of Honor page; Rattlesnake Wisdom from Squawville; and Out in the Big Open.

Another section, titled "Southwest Quarter," listed such things as forty acres of "Historical Matter, Anecdotes, Stories," written by those who were themselves tillers of the soil and reapers of the harvest. The "North 80" section pertains to literary and artistic thoughts from personal viewpoints, stressing the clippings from other sources. The "160-Acre Homestead" includes philosophical smatterings such as Greasewood Preaching, Sagebrush Clippings, Yucca Round Table, and Gunnysack to Ermine. The page ends with "640 Acres of Wholesome News." The magazines do not seem maudlin as you read them; they were really an effort to leave history to future generations as well as to compliment and give thorough thumb-nail sketches of actual life on the Mojave. The love of the Mojave Desert runs through like a needed thread to pin-point the era.

The avowed purpose of the magazine was "to boost the fairest section of earth given by nature to man to till and cultivate and in the end to reap a reward of golden harvests of grain and fruits — the Desert in the southeastern part of California." It had no politics. Its religion was the "open one practised in the hills, vales and plains, recognizing no creed, faith, ritual, doctrine or dogma, merely trying to support all that is good. . ."

The periodical also had practical thoughts — it wanted the world to know the desert was there, and boost both the desert and San Bernardino County. It felt there was "nothing known to agriculture that would not grow there" — it just needed water, which it assured was abundant. Wrote the editor: "The soil, alluvial and volcanic ash and enriched by the bones of animals and birds for thousands of years is such that when once ripped open by the plow and the seed planted, it will give to the husbandman a return that can be equaled in no corner of the great world."

Penny Morrow of Oro Grande was one of the instigators of the magazine. It can be said of the little magazine, that the residents were sincere, and believed all they wrote. There are some interesting stories of the ranches, telling how they were planned, and what they were doing in the efforts to colonize and make the desert really blossom as in the legendary words, "like the rose." There were biographical sketches of such people as Arthur E. Hull, who as a capitalist and promoter, living in Los Angeles and Escondido, invested in land in Apple Valley, built a veritable show place for a desert home and was the first president of the Victor Valley Chamber of Commerce. His wife was the daughter of Joseph Farminich, sugar beet king of Buffalo, New York, who was the first man in the United States to manufacture glucose, and whose son, George Farminich, a few years later, added to his father's business the largest cornstarch factory in the world. Mrs. Hull, a beautiful and charming person, did a great deal to promote the desert.

Social leaders from the outside world came to live on the desert on homesteads. Many of them were women who had wealth and influence and fine social standing. Some of them came for health reasons, others, for the love of the desert. The issues read like an historical "who's who" and many fine old family names are listed in the three editions.

In one issue there is a picture of Miss Carrie Bennette, owner of the Cottonwood Bennette Ranch, who was "social and equestrian queen of the Mojave." She was loved and adored by everyone, from the smallest tot to the oldest resident. She could rope any animal that moved, from a panther to a baby coyote. She held the championship in Southern California as a bronco lariatist.

There was Mrs. John T. Bennette who was called the "first lady of Oro Grande," a handsome thirty-five-year-old woman who had the distinction of being the most highly educated woman in San Bernardino County at that time. There was the Turner family whose ranch near Victorville was the historical landmark site of the last stage station. These were some of the substantial citizens in the "Kingdom."

Transcontinental trains whizzed through the region and the passengers could get glimpses of ranch houses and grounds from the train. An early writer likened the scene to the phrase much used in that era — "That's out where the West begins!"

One issue reveals that the King ranch was to be subdivided into thirty-two twenty-acre apple orchards. Mrs. Sarah J. Cheney, beautiful white-haired owner of Bide-A-Wee Ranch, was a society leader who went to the desert for her health. Her nearest neighbor was Mrs. Francis A. Corwin of the Sun Kist Ranch who had reigned socially elsewhere. They filed on adjoining claims and became "dwellers of the desert." Forsaking their social pasts, these two women, no longer young, cleared, plowed, and cultivated their sixty acres of the valley's finest land. They built roads and planted fruit trees and windbreaks. They were active in the Sunrise Valley Improvement Association, the Yucca Social Club, and the Yucca Round Table. The latter group pledged itself to build a home for "broken and superannuated writers and artists," to be called "The Artists' and Authors' Desert Eyrie," and was to be built on the Suaslika Ranch in Sunrise Valley.

It is like looking at an old family album to scan the pictorial pages of "The Album of the Fair" in the old magazine issues and note the trend of women's dress; the cowboy outfits of the younger ones; the western working garb of the men. It is interesting to read of the women who kept the community life rolling and the men who were empire-minded.

And now to close the pages of *The Kingdom of the Sun* with its Camera Chats; its Life-O-Graphs; its sub-

A Scene on the J. T. Bennette Ranch at Oro Grande, about 1913
A sketch by William C. Leone, from an old photograph which appeared as an

scribing readers all over America; its articles and poems by John Steven McGroarty, California's "poet laureate," historian and author; the beautiful poems; the old pictures and outmoded type. The pages have been enlightening of the Mojave River story.

Hesperia, Oro Grande, Victorville, Apple Valley, the numerous ranches — too many to gather for this volume — round out an interesting history of the desert. It is all a record — in story, poetry and picture — of the building of an empire valley. That the empire did not materialize as an entity at the time does not matter. Foundations were laid for the decades to come.

15

Barstow Between-the-Tracks

Let not our town be large remembering
That little Athens was the Muses' home,
That Oxford rules the heart of London still,
That Florence gave the Renaissance to Rome.
Record it for the grandson of your son—
A city was not builded in a day;
Our little town cannot complete her soul
Till countless generations pass away.

Nicholas Vachel Lindsay,
from *On the Building of Springfield*

Barstow was named for William Barstow Strong, president of the Santa Fe Railroad at the time its tracks were laid through the Mojave Desert. The coming of the railroad occasioned the founding of the town. Daggett had made a bid for this railroad center, but it set an exhorbitant price for its land and it lost out.

In its beginnings Barstow lay in the lowlands of the river. In earlier times the Indians had camped in the area, using an existing high red-brown promontory as a lookout. This high bluff is called Buzzard's Rock. Long after the Indians left the area, the spot was used for summer picnics. A business section and a few homes were built as the railroad came through. In time, the town expanded along the tracks and there was a great deal of activity. Before the site became settled, it had been on the trail of the pioneers. Fish Pond, while not in the area of present-day Barstow, was at one time the only settlement for miles around. Fish Pond was also the settlement point for the activities up and down the river until the days of the coming of the railroad.

Fish Pond was the site of a store where provisions could be bought by emigrants, and where horses could be fed and shod. Lafayette Meacham owned and operated this small mercantile business. Fish Pond was located, just east of Barstow, on what is now the Marine Corps Depot of Supplies near Daggett. The point that became Barstow was a few miles to the west. Meacham's home was in San Bernardino. It was one of his sons who participated in the discovery of silver in the Calico Mountains. At some time before the discovery, Meacham was out chasing an Indian whom he had seen stealing one of his horses. His chase led him into a defile in the colored hills. As it was beginning to get dark, he decided not to take the risk of going any further. He did not want to lose another horse, nor his own life.

Intent on finding his horse, Meacham only casually noted a high ledge that he recalled years later as being red-capped with bands on it. He made a mental note to tell his sons about it and returned to his store.

Another area that was a site for settlement of the desert area that was to become Barstow, was Grapevine Station, a stop on the railroad line. The site was owned by Ellis Miller and was located where today's Fort Irwin road branches north. Near this station was the old abandoned Lee Mine. It had been worked spasmodically by a man named Lee who was constantly showing specimens which he called "white lead." Little attention was

SUNRISE CANYON IN THE CALICO HILLS

The canyon took its name from the radiant colors of the rock in these hills where silver was found in 1881, leading to settlement of Yermo, Daggett and Barstow

paid to his specimens or his chatter. He eventually left the region and the mine was forgotten.

A desert valley rancher near the site of future Barstow, Robert W. Waterman (who was to become governor of California), stopped at Miller's Grapevine Station one day. Miller, knowing Waterman was interested in mining, suggested that the latter investigate the old Lee Mine. Waterman did and made a nice strike in silver. That was in the fall of 1880. Later, the name of Grapevine was changed to Waterman Junction, which for a time was the name of early Barstow. His strike started a prospecting fever which culminated in the discovery of rich silver mines in the Calico hills and mountains.

Barstow became quite a busy little town and people started moving in. It lay there on the river bed near accepted trails. The railroad had made the greatest of impressions on those few early settlements as they were the centers where people paused. A depot was constructed and eventually a Harvey House was established. Quite a number of business houses (including several saloons) were operating to take care of the emigrants who were still rolling over the desert.

The Barstovians dropped all the early names it had gathered as it grasped for identity, and it was fast taking on an entity of its own. Later the great diesel shops at Barstow were to assure the town's permanency.

An active chamber of commerce was formed in 1907. The members had visions of growth, but little did they realize that a few decades later their highway would take thousands of people daily through the town which would one day expand beyond the tracks and the river bed.

The chamber had only about fifty-five cents in its exchequer at the time, and had started making plans for something of a social nature to bring in some revenue. The Harvey House promised to provide a banquet for the sum of one dollar and fifty cents per person (a really expensive affair for that day) and the caterer promised not only to provide the dinner, but to make it a dinner to end all dinners.

To start with, it took money to put on a dinner to make money. Lubin Henderson, who operated his men's clothing store down by the tracks, had business in Los Angeles. He was only recently from Scotland and had an appointment in the southern city to receive his final papers of naturalization. Accompanied by a friend, he left for Los Angeles.

In the name of the Barstow Chamber of Commerce, the pair from the desert outpost looked at some really nice (and expensive) invitations and menus. No definite date had been set for the dinner, so the desert men set a date right then and there. They took full responsibility for the payment of the purchase. It was upon their return to Barstow that they learned of the pitiful balance in the chamber's treasury.

However, the committee from the chamber got busy and canvassed the town and community for a hundred diners. The three saloon-keepers, most prosperous of the businessmen, were each delivered twenty tickets at the price of three dollars each. The chamber pocketed the sixty dollars from each saloon-keeper whose tickets were to be sold or given away. With the sale of the sixty tickets the promoters had one hundred and eighty dollars, and a bright and hopeful future for their money-making plans. The rest of the tickets were sold and the banquet was assured.

One hundred and fifty guests attended the affair. One hundred had menus and invitational tickets. The remainder of the guests were passed on into the dining-room when they paid for their dinners. The banquet was the social highlight of Barstow. There were speakers and a toastmaster — and everything!

Obtaining a county bridge over the Mojave River was the next project for the Chamber of Commerce. Representatives from the Santa Fe Railroad, county officials, and the committee from the chamber walked untold miles along the river to decide upon the location of the bridge they were asking for. They chose a location where the water span was narrow. The bridge was constructed and the chamber turned its activities to new problems.

Barstow's life history has been rather thoroughly involved with railroad development. Looking at the great network of railway tracks in the bottomland where the town had its beginnings, one can fully realize that it is one of the great railroad division points of the Southwest.

In use until 1966 at the Barstow railroad office, was a small brass impression stamp which inscribed "C. S. R. R., Waterman Junction" which made countless documents official. These initials stood for California Southern Railroad.

Fires, which often ravage pioneer towns, took their toll in Barstow-between-the-tracks. In 1906 the west end of the town was destroyed by flames. It was a $100,000 fire, and started from a leak in a gasoline lamp at a barber stop in the Sloan and Hart building, a two-story structure which was occupied by a saloon and barber shop on the ground floor, and a rooming-house above. The building was practically new, the furniture for the rooming-house unpacked in the rear of the building.

The next few years other fires followed: the east side, including the Harvey House, the depot, a lodging-house and many dugouts which were used for rooms. When the roundhouse burned (where there was a well) there was not a drop of water available to use in putting out the fire. Fire struck again in 1921, taking a drug store, a butcher shop, a hotel, a rooming-house, a grocery store and the post office. By then there were some insurance policies available, though the premiums were very high. In another year the business area was again hit by fire, taking some of the newer buildings that had been built to replace buildings lost in the former fire.

The story is told of a leading citizen who was like an old fire-horse and could never resist going to a fire. Whenever he knew there was a fire he grabbed a Santa Fe hose cart at one of the company houses, tied it to his automobile and sped to the scene of the fire. In one special case, when he arrived at the fire all he had following him was the handle of the cart. The Santa Fe fire chief "cussed him out pretty thoroughly" for using the company's cart. The best part of the story is that the leading citizen's wife had already put out the fire with a garden hose. This leading citizen was the late Gene White, Barstow druggist for many years.

There have been times in the past when it was difficult at Barstow to cross the river, which is often quite wide when floods are rampaging. There were hazardous places to cross then. Quick-sands threatened as they did one time when the waters were high and the undertaker went across with a wagon drawn by horses, taking the body of a man to the undertaking parlor. The liveryman led the way for the wagon, but in mid-stream the horses went down. People came on horseback and the water-flooded wagon was finally hauled out of the spot.

Barstow's early residents were thoughtful of automobile travelers. Having experienced many difficult phases of desert living in pioneer days, they knew the hazards of automobiles on desert roads. When a car left Las Vegas someone would telegraph to Barstow that the car had started. If it did not arrive in due time, a search was begun. The sands then, as now, were tricky.

About 1925 Barstow moved "up the hill," on the mesa-land above the river bed. This allowed for expansion of the railroad yards which were a big item for Barstow's prosperity.

16

Southwest Quarter of Section Six

Be favorable to bold beginnings.

Virgil, from *Georgics*

Perhaps the most colorful of all of Barstow's early settlers was Charlie Williams. The foundation of Barstow-on-the-mesa was begun by a quarrel over two-bits (twenty-five cents!) and Charlie was a resulting beneficiary of it.

In the beginning, Barstow-on-the-mesa was a homesteading community. In the year 1907, there were saloons in Barstow — down in Barstow-between-the-tracks. There were a few other buildings tucked in among the railroad establishments. This first section of Barstow was built in the river bottomland. Harry Workman, who tended bar in the Mosley Saloon, and the Santa Fe agent, a man named Hutchison, had heard that the southwest quarter of section six was to be opened for homesteading. Each decided to get to Los Angeles as fast as he could to file on it.

Hutchison was ahead of Workman, but there was a train wreck and Workman got to the city before Hutchison did and filed on the land. So Workman had the first house in Barstow-on-the-mesa.

Charlie Williams (as he tells it)[1] was about to take

---

[1] Caryl Kronser, "Pioneer Tells All on Birth of Barstow," in *Printer-Review,* Nov. 15, 1945, and July 17, 1947, as dictated by Charlie Williams to the editor.

off and shake the sand of Barstow off his shoes. He stood in the doorway of the Sloan & Hart Saloon, his hat on his head, and drunk as usual, waiting for a freight train to "ride the rods." He was evidently in from the mines and ready to drift.

As he stood there he heard Sloan arguing with his bartender, Joe Holbook, "over a two-bit difference at the register." According to Charlie, they were good friends and both honest "to the core," and that it was "just one of those feverish things that caused a heated moment that spilled the beans." Sloan noticed Charlie standing in the doorway and turned to him and said, "You tend bar while I go get someone." Then as an after-thought said, "Hell, no, I'll work on this side." He persuaded Charlie to take over. It was just Charlie's luck that the beer keg ran out and he had to tap a new one.

He didn't know how — he was only used to drinking the contents. It was the old style beer keg which had to be pounded with a wooden mallet. If it were hit too often (which Charlie did) the spigot flew out.

Said Charlie, "I'll tell you Niagara Falls was a dusty spot compared to that barroom."

When he had gone behind the bar he hadn't meant to stay very long, so he still had his hat on. Let Charlie tell this:

> . . . There was foam dripping off the ceiling, off my hat, foam all over that bar and floor. John Sloan grabbed the tub and saved half the keg. John looked me over thoughtfully and said I guess you'll do.
>
> I worked for him for four years and in the meantime southwest quarter of section six, called the town of Barstow, is here now all due to a dispute over two-bits.

One day when Charlie was working in the cellar of the saloon, his friend, Harry Workman, who had been successful in filing on his homestead on the mesa, came in and told Charlie that he had quarreled with his boss and he wanted to pull out. He wanted to relinquish his homestead and asked Charlie to buy it. Charlie answered that he had no money. Sloan, who heard the conversation, said casually to Charlie, "Go to the safe and help yourself to the money."

Charlie did just that and for $250 of borrowed money became the possessor of southwest quarter of section six—upon which the town of Barstow was built. In his interview with the editor of the Barstow paper[2] Charlie said:

> Harry had not completed his homestead nor sub-divided it. It was Charlie Williams that sub-divided the town and I would not have done this except for my wife. It was Mrs. Williams that is responsible for the development of the new town. Otherwise as a hobo miner I would have left the town and never completed homesteading the property.

According to Charlie his wife was the first woman to live in Barstow; she was formerly Mrs. Sarah Albright and had come there to teach school.

Charlie offered his boss, John Sloan, the whole quarter. Sloan said he wouldn't spit on the land. Six months later, Charlie sold Sloan three lots for $250 each. The Williams Addition was the first subdivision in Barstow. There is a long list of the people who bought lots of Charlie. They are listed in the Barstow *Printer-Review*.[3]

A part of the property on which the Barstow High

[2] *Ibid.*   [3] *Ibid.*

School stands is included in the Williams quarter. Among the purchasers were Ed and Ella Pitcher. Ed Pitcher was a twenty-mule-team driver of the early days in the desert. He is said to have been one of the best drivers of that famous mode of transportation, and drove for ten years.

Mrs. Pitcher was the former Ella Connor who came west from Oklahoma to visit her brother, Mike Connor, who was an early resident of the pioneer days in Barstow. Mike lived down in the clustered area in the lowlands of old Barstow. When the railroad was built through the region to haul borax from the Calico mines about ten miles distant, Ed went to work for the railroad. Later, he became town constable. The Pitchers bought the Inez Hotel, Barstow's finest hotel of the early days.

During Ella's early married life she was considered the best-dressed woman west of Albuquerque. She carved a diverse life for herself on the desert, and in her adopted desert town of Barstow. She was census taker, social worker, railroad clerk, food administrator during World War I, Red Cross worker, bond saleslady, realtor, and during her husband's work as constable was deputized to assist him. Her early ambition had been to study law, but her marriage cancelled that.

When Barstow moved up on the mesa, the Pitchers moved their home and another house they owned, up from the tracks in the river bottom lands. She celebrated her ninetieth birthday in 1967. Mrs. Pitcher is now residing in Victorville.

The first lot that Charlie Williams sold went to Donald C. Henderson of Needles, California, on August 3,

Mrs. ELLA PITCHER AND A TWENTY-MULE-TEAM BORAX FREIGHTER

Ella Connor came to Barstow from Indian Territory at the age of sixteen in 1896. She met and married Ed Pitcher, an early-day twenty-mule-team driver, who pos-

1910. The property is described as Lot 8, Block 9, on Williams Street, west of First Street. This lot sold for $250 which funded repayment of the loan from his boss, John Sloan. In later years, this and other lots sold for thousands of dollars.

One of Charlie's deals over his homesteaded property was quite interesting. A certain oil company had repeatedly offered Charlie and Mrs. Williams $12,500 for two lots on Main Street, in downtown Barstow, but Charlie refused to sell to the firm.

Again, let Charlie tell about this deal himself:

> In April of 1932, while in Los Angeles, I dropped in at the (oil) company office. The manager was very glad to see me and invited me into his private office. He pulled open a drawer and offered me some of his private stock. We talked a while and he again urged me to sell the corner lots for $12,500. We talked a while more and he poured me another generous drink.
>
> "I'll tell you what I'll do," I said—"You give me $11,000 cash right now and I'll give you title to those two lots." He said that was impossible, he had no authority to make cash payments of that size, it would have to (be) authorized by higher sources, and (they) would pay $12,500 for the lots.
>
> "You give me $11,000 cash right now and I'll sell; otherwise I won't sell at any price." Well, they wanted the location and he burned up the wires to San Francisco and San Francisco phoned New York. He got the authorization, phoned the bank to hold open after closing hours, went down to the bank and returned with $11,000 in greenbacks.
>
> "How did you like the drinks, Charlie?" he asked after the money was paid over.
>
> "Darn good," I said. "They cost me $750 a drink."
>
> Well, I put the money in a grocery sack and went to San Bernardino. I took in all the dives where they would murder a man for two bits; laid the grocery sack with the $11,000

cash on the bar, and ordered drinks. After spending a couple of days carrying the grocery sack around San Bernardino, I returned to Barstow and had some more drinks.[4]

Once when Charlie was running an oil service station a limousine drove up and a smartly dressed man asked where the Harvey House was. Charlie told him:

.   .   . go a thousand feet east, turn right, go by the stockyards, turn right, then take the other road but turn left, then turn right, continue to where there was a turn but not take that but turn left and keep going and there's the Harvey House—you can't miss it.

As Charlie said, "You won't believe this, but I'm giving you the facts and nothing but the facts." In twenty minutes the man was back and said, "Where did you send me? I wound up at the round house."

Charlie gave the directions all over again. In a half hour the man was back again. Charlie closed the station and went with him. His lost friend was the "biggest oil man in the country."

Although Charlie Williams would have been a bum the rest of his life if it had not been for Mrs. Williams, he had a lot of faith in Barstow. He was assured there was a world of materials around Barstow that the United States was crying for. Chief among the minerals spoken of was bentonite.

Charlie liked the climate, and he complimented his wife by using the pronoun "we." As he said so many times, "I take no credit for the founding of the town of

---

[4] The story of Charlie Williams won a one-hundred-dollar Victory Bond for being the best feature story published in any Southern California community newspaper during 1945.

Barstow, it is all due to my wife, Sarah Williams. Without her I would have been a hobo miner and drifter."

Charlie Williams was more than a bartender and the
founder of a town. He was a philosopher. Deep in his
heart he loved beauty. Hobo-mining must have made
him an observant man. Somewhere along the line between his hobo jaunts, Charlie came alive to an interest
in the mysteries of rocks and minerals. They fascinated
him. He enjoyed them — liked working with them in
his lapidary shop. He was akin to the Bard in his belief
that every stone held a sermon. He would pick up a
specimen, hold it gently in his hand, and say, "There's
a sermon in every stone, if you know how to look for it."

In an interview Charlie said:

> This smooth, round bit from the bottom of a deep shaft
> brings the message that thousands of years ago this par-
> ticular stratum was the bed of a rolling torrent. At another
> level the pink, petrified roots of the palm, bear record of a
> tropical age, while the track of a three-toed horse embedded
> near by, in what was once clay, conjures up visions of a
> prehistoric horse snorting through tropical foliage where
> sandy waters now reach to the horizon.
> . . . when I look at crystals of quartz or galena or
> gold and see how the agitated atom and molecules have
> settled down to definite but individual patterns, I realize
> that there is a guiding hand back of all this.[5]

Charlie Williams, the hobo-miner, had followed the
trail of the will-o'-the-wisps from Alaska to Mexico, so
he had a varied opportunity to learn of rocks and minerals. He liked his rocks with colors in them. He pos-

---

[5]Cora Keagle, "Charley Williams—of the Calico Hills," in *Desert Magazine*, March 1943. The different spellings of the given nickname of Williams
are according to the use by the authors cited.

sessed about every hue ever embedded in rock. He liked his crystals best. They intrigued him. As it was with his land affairs, Mrs. Williams was right there along with him, steady and pat, and very English.

The Williams' collection of rocks and minerals took many honors — blue ribbons, cups, sweepstakes and trophies around the country.

When he first began collecting, he was hobo-mining, so most of his early collections went by the wayside. When he found "colorful Calico" he "lingered a while," for Calico and its bright hills brought many specimens. Then he met Mrs. Williams and he lingered longer. He was a dedicated rockhound, a sound philosopher, a good bartender and a town founder, all due to Mrs. Williams, of course!

Flood Waters Make a Mile-wide Stream at Barstow's Big Spanned Bridge

This fine bridge, built in 1931, has withstood the flood waters

17

Growing Pains from a Morgue

The news! Our morning, noon and evening cry;
  Day unto day repeats it 'til we die.

Charles Sprague, from *Curiosity*

From out of the files of the first newspaper in Barstow has been gleaned some of the happenings showing the spirit of the little desert outpost that refused to stay a mining supply center, but which reached out with grasping arms for life.

Back in 1910, when Barstow had its first weekly news sheet, there appeared many interesting comments on the town's hopes for a better future. The editor, speaking in behalf of the people of his hamlet, was concerned one spring day about the bridge that crossed the Mojave River. (He spelled it with an "h"—Mohave.) He thought the bridge should be put in condition before the high water came again, for it was a flood year for the Mojave River Valley. The flood waters played havoc around Barstow. The concrete pier on the east end of the wagon bridge was underscoured and settled about three feet.

Street improvement was a burning question for the city-makers that year. From one issue that spring came the following:

Barstow's streets should be leveled and oiled—as supervisors do in the orange section. The county derives enough revenue from Barstow and the desert to give more attention to road improvments. With oil selling at 30 cents a barrel in Bakersfield (across the Tehachapis) the supervisors could afford to put some oil on Barstow's streets. We are weary of the dust. Barstow wants better streets and road conditions. A better road up the valley to Victorville is also needed.

So there was a troubled cry, editorially, for oil on troublesome dust and a bridge over troubled waters.

Fifty years ago, Barstow was already envisioning the expansion of the desert — and trying to get ready for it. An editorial went, in part,

> If Barstow were a county seat it would be easier for all the desert people to see the records, and the money collected from the desert would be spent here. The money spent by the traveling county officers, coroner, sheriff and prisoners, school superintendent and others would be cut down.

County division reared its complex head:

> County division was much discussed in Victorville since last issue of PRINTER. The only county official ever selected or allowed to be nominated from the desert was Dr. H. Pittman for coroner, and yet they all want our votes. The desert part of this county calls for a different form of government than that in existence, and in the southwest part of the county conditions do not apply to the desert at all.

The town of Daggett, about eight miles below Barstow, a supply town during the Calico boom in the 'eighties, also went on record that year as in favor of county division. A great deal of publicity was given the idea. In fact, proposals were drawn up and presented to the voters through the medium of the newspaper. Barstow was obtaining stature.

The following digest from the *Printer*, gives a thumbnail sketch of the policy presented:

A petition must be presented to the board of supervisors, describing boundaries of a proposed new county, the population of the new, and what would be left of the old has to be presented. The petition to be signed by 65 percent of qualified electors of proposed new county and 50 percent of those of the territory which would be left in the old after the new county was formed. Boundaries of new counties cannot pass within five miles of the county seat of the old county, nor can a county be formed that has a population less than 10,000, nor where the formation of new county would reduce the population of the old county to less than 2,000. Reference was made to page 194, Statute of 1909, chapter 123.

San Bernardino County is the largest county in the United States. But, said an editor, "Big counties are not always governed for the best interests of the sparsely settled section." "Too often" he added thoughtfully, "the county seat absorbs the taxes and licenses, and the county districts get few roads or returns."

The next June hopeful news commented: "A bank at Barstow would get much business from subdividing the county."

In July of that year the Van Dyke Ranch, which had been established since 1902, had just "harvested the second cutting of alfalfa and baled the crop which has yielded four tons per acre."

It is hoped that this was not a common occurrence: "The coroner has been sitting on the body of an old man found dead and half eaten by coyotes. The body lay under the bridge there for some time."

Railroad history at Barstow was recorded: The Santa Fe had a twenty-stall roundhouse with turntable, office and store building. Space was reserved for steam, electric and machine tool plants. The steam plant consisted of one locomotive and two Scotch marine boilers. Light-plant-one had a high speed auto engine and electric generator, switchboard appliances, office and company buildings. Staff, eighty to one hundred and ten men, and four hundred to six hundred engines were turned per month, inspected and repaired. They had large and powerful engines: Number 1700 was largest in the world. By the end of the 1940s, Barstow's Santa Fe Diesel Shops were considered the largest in the country, one of the factors which kept Barstow on the map in big, black letters.

Said the paper, which had become the *Printer-Review*: "Settlers and farmers are crowding the cattle back." The paper listed the following cattle owners in the region: Rock Springs Cattle Company of Kelso (beyond Soda Lake), 8,000; S. E. Yates, 800; Van Dyke Ranch, 200; L. C. Starkey, 800; Rancho Verde (Victorville), 4,500; Box S Ranch, 3,500; Las Flores, 1,000; Martin McInnis, 160; Miss Carrie E. Bennette, 400.

March, 1911: A census had been taken in the Mojave Valley. Barstow boasted 1,066 inhabitants, becoming the metropolis even then along the river. Victorville ranked second with 480, and Oro Grande, over in the "Kingdom of the Sun," was beginning to shine with 280 cheerful folks. Hesperia, nine miles up the river from Victorville towards the mesa, had only 42 people. Yermo, down the other way, was not listed. It had been quite a town during the Calico boom; possibly it was making up its mind whether it would go "ghost" or stay in circulation. Out at Silver Lake in the Mojave Sink country there were 135 people.

That spring, ranchers on the river were connecting their wells with Mojave River channels to secure an ample water supply.

Citizens were again scratching their heads over "home rule." They were asking for candidates for supervisor from within their boundaries to cut out "interferences of the San Bernardino machine." And they were successful eventually.

Desert land claims got prominent coverage: A new rule by the Secretary of the Interior relieved entrymen of irrigating an entire claim. One-eighth must be cultivated, with water brought in by ditches to the rest.

In April, over 10,000 fruit trees were reported received in Victorville, up the valley about thirty miles, which ye editor thought showed the faith of many new settlers in the desert as a fruit country. One colony set out eighty acres in fruit, putting up fences.

Over at Yermo two hundred pear trees had been set out at the Tom Williams Ranch, later to be the site on which annual "Calico Days" is held when the Old West is relived by the people of the lower valley.

From out of the yellowed pages of the old news sheets came this snake-bite remedy which was recommended by Dr. Sam M. Slocum, "eminent physician" who had spent many years in "mining on the desert" and who always carried it with him. He is reported to have saved twelve lives with it. Here it is:

Two ounce vial of ammonia to apply freely to bite wound after opening and squeezing out poison. Saturate the wound thoroughly for two hours or more to neutralize poison. If wound on arm or leg, ligature belt or cord twisted tightly between wound and heart to prevent poison reaching blood vessels and vital parts. After treatment of two or three hours, wound should be cauterized by burning small amount of gunpowder on it and searing with hot nail or iron to prevent blood poisoning. Hypodermic syringe gives quicker application of remedy if use is understood.

That summer Barstow advertised for a dentist. Said the paper: "He should make headquarters here and reach out for business."

In June of 1911, Mrs. Ella Pitcher, one of Barstow's most important citizens and its oldest citizen in length of years, was reported to have found it necessary to return from San Francisco to get warm.

The *Printer-Review* editor was, with a vengeance, advocating woman suffrage. This, with a sidelight on human rights, was the subject of an editorial that August: ". . . Mrs. Potts financed the big cement plant at Oro Grande and hundreds of California women have shown ability in business, law, art, science." He couldn't let it rest:

Why are they not competent to vote? Thousands have property and should be given the ballot to protect their interests.

If it is all right to induce them to invest their money in mines and other desert enterprises, why not give them a voice in the laws to govern? Suffrage should be taken away from a lot of men and given to women. Dictatorial men should not vote on it. Women should settle the question among themselves.

Daggett was there all the time. In 1912 the paper had this headline: DAGGETT OLD BOYS. Then the editor commented: "Most of the fellows who left Calico went direct to Heaven, but a few failed to leave their addresses."

On to 1913: Barstow was improving. A telephone system went in, with 32 'phones in operation. Leona Mitchell was the "hello girl."

In April the paper was concerned over the burro situation:

> If the people of Barstow ever expect to make a shady green spot in the desert, it is time something was done to abate the nuisance. 'Overgrown rats' foil efforts of many to make a place worth living in.
>
> Broken fences and gates—through barbed-wire—peeled bark from trees, eating the buds, killing them and bringing to nought the efforts in money and time spent by many of our enterprising citizens who have tried to make a green spot in this desert.
>
> Present law does not permit animals to roam at large without a keeper.
>
> Damages may be collected from the owner of animals which are allowed to roam onto private property. But the burro is not worth one-tenth the damage it can do in a half hour.

In May: "The first supervisorial district went wet." Business in Barstow suspended. Hottest wet and dry fight that ever happened.

And today: Barstow has its good streets. A fine bridge spans the river. There has been a succession of supervisors from the desert—and the county *is still undivided.*

18

Outpost of Empire

*To those who come to the desert with friendliness
it gives friendship; to those who come with courage
it gives new strength of character.
Those seeking relaxation find release from the
world of man-made troubles. For those seeking beauty
the desert offers nature's rarest artistry.
This is the desert men and women love.*

Randall Henderson,
from *Desert Magazine*

Barstow people like to say their little city is a "town in the desert" rather than a "desert town." There seems to be a world of difference in the two outlooks.

A desert town, they say, is one that emerges from the surroundings as the result of a natural cause, such as the discovery of a mineral lode, and remains alive as long as the reasons for its inception continue. When those reasons are gone it becomes shrouded in past happenings and is styled a ghost town. A town in the desert is one that grows because people want to live in the desert, stay in the place of their choosing, push the hopes and dreams for growth, and remain to see the results and to enjoy life. Barstow, they claim, is in this category.

Barstow citizens like to tell of the man from the East; fresh from the East. Getting out of his car, he walked to the sidewalk curbing. Stretching the kinks of travel out of his arms he said to someone standing near, "So this is a desert town!" He had passed low, squatty buildings. He had driven through clouds of dust. Vagrant winds had picked up fine sand and made yellow spirals in the air as he drove along the highway flanking the washes that took care of overflow water from the Mojave River. He had despaired of reaching the end of the many desert miles before he reached the spreading town that had once been but a desert outpost catering to miners. A town, he thought, even in the late 1940s, that was only a place to get through and on to somewhere else as quickly as possible.

"A desert town!" he echoed himself.

"Wrong for once, stranger," he heard someone say. "This is a town in the desert."

Stranger wanted to know the difference. Proudly the citizen said, "A desert town is one that can pull up stakes overnight and vanish. Such as Calico was—the old mining camp. Like a lot of mining camps all over the state."

Barstow, a town *in* the desert, started primarily, he said, as a supply town and graduated to a railroad town. Back in 1885, he told the stranger, there was nothing here but the desert and a railroad track coming down into the Mojave. The next year a new line brought more trains over Cajon Pass. In another year a Harvey House was established and a railroad station took form. Thus Barstow began. It had all the desert to spread out in, with plenty of space to grow in and on.

The stranger was converted and became a citizen. He became one of the populace, understanding the vagaries,

even the fact that the Mojave River itself was unorthodox. He learned to understand the people who had lived
in the river town over a period of years. Understood
why they were content to stay in the desert and far from
metropolitan places. He got used to the howl of the
coyotes from beyond the fringes of town. At first he
noticed only the pungent smell of the creosote that
grew in his yard, then he became so accustomed to it
he knew it was as much a part of the area as were the
very blue skies, and the barren hills. Too, he learned
to take the great distances in his stride.

He liked the nonchalance of the desert people: their
dress — blue jeans or formal attire; their indifference to
rank or money as such; their independence; doing what
they wanted to do, choosing their friends for their own
particular reasons; their enjoyment of life; their deliber-
ation in living.

The new citizen took a practical look at his new
country. He found that Barstow has always been a
natural supply town for the mining industry, and that
metallic and non-metallic elements and minerals have
been found in the mountains and hills that surround this
desert locality. He was amazed at the interesting things
he was learning.

Before World War ii, Barstow had been essentially a
railroad town with a population of around twenty-five
hundred. It seemed to burst out overnight as a military
center. During the war it had four government posts
radiating in every direction. It is now the homesite for
the large Marine Corps Supply Depot and Fort Irwin,
both of which have expanded greatly since the war closed.

The diesel shops that have been established at Barstow account for a great increase in population. The railroad brings a large payroll to the little city.

Barstow is situated near the geographic center of the great Mojave Desert. It is nestled in the middle valley of the Mojave Desert, practically in the shadow of the beautiful Calico hills and mountains. There are many places of scenic interest for sightseeing.

Geological formations, fossil beds, Joshua trees, wildflower sweeps, interesting old mines, and a rockhound's paradise are among the features that beckon people to the area for weekends and vacations.

Barstow's past, starting down in the lowlands, had been plenty rowdy and rollicking. It has always been bravely a town that had what it wanted. Its days of "wine, women and song" have been as individual as those of other mining camps or western outposts.

Good roads, fine homes, a splendid class of people, thriving businesses, group organizations of every kind, churches, excellent schools and transcontinental railroads have made it a cosmopolitan community.

Coming into Barstow at night, or standing on a knoll somewhere on the town's outskirts, this little city built on hillslopes presents such a sparkling view that it has appropriately been spoken of as a "city of jewels." This was especially true during World War ii for Barstow never had a blackout; its neon signs shone like banners throughout the war nights.

From Barstow's heights fine panoramas are seen. The long line of the river with its green, lush trees and thickets which stay green for so long a time in the desert; the colored hills on every side; the neon lights that still go on each night as they did in World War ii; the lines of moving automobiles along the main streets and freeway; the gray desert hills whose sides and ravines are dotted with desert holly and other plants in hundreds of species — it all speaks of the river basin that has created a way of life all its own along its wayward course.

Many years ago Barstow began attempts to incorporate as a city. The fight was long and stubborn. World War ii postponed the dream. When the war was over, interested parties wanted to see the little town in the desert complete its incorporation plans. The issue was kept before the people constantly. On September 30, 1947, the incorporation became a fact.

Barstow is a gateway to many places, in many directions. It has a great pioneer history and it has a great natural history. It has long since lost its title of desert outpost. It is now an empire. It has come a long way since it was Barstow-between-the-tracks to being Barstow-on-the-hill — the hill that Charlie and Mrs. Williams homesteaded and which started with a quarrel over two-bits.

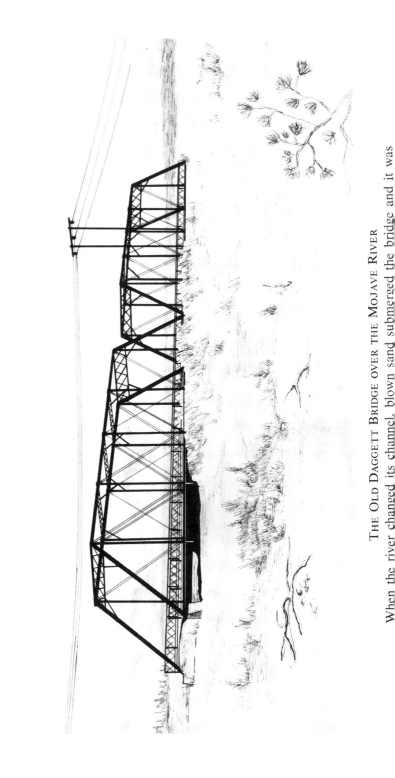

THE OLD DAGGETT BRIDGE OVER THE MOJAVE RIVER

When the river changed its channel, blown sand submerged the bridge and it was

19

Daggett Was a Man's Town

The man is richest whose pleasures are the cheapest.

Henry David Thoreau,
from his *Journal*, March 11, 1836

Daggett, lively camp of the 'eighties when Calico was producing silver and borate, was distinctively a man's town. Less than ten miles down the river from the future town of Barstow, Daggett attracted many men to the Calico silver mines, and the later borate interests. Sooner or later they were there: the desert roamers, miners, prospectors, promoters, gamblers, traders, adventurers, and floaters.

There were no mines at Daggett; it served only as an outfitting center for the mines and for shipping ore. Primarily because of the mines, and objectively because the river was there, the people came. Water solved so many problems on the desert. It was a site suitable for a rendezvous, reminiscent of the days of the trappers and explorers. Here the men could relax when they came in from the mines where they worked hard and long. Here they could go on a spree if that was what they wanted, and no one thought anything about it one way or another.

Daggett has been described by old-timers as a shabby, dreary little town, sprawled out on both sides of the railroad tracks. The tracks were the center of a four-hundred-foot right-of-way that divided the town. The south side was the residential area — the business firms took the north side.

In its peak there were about fifty homes and shacks. Most of them were made of rough boards standing on end, with slats nailed over the cracks. Only a few were ever painted. Most of them were weathered and drab-looking. Some were finished inside by cheese-cloth covered over with paper. The desert can be a windy country at times and the early settlers must have had their souls tried deeply in the thrown-together shacks with no means of shutting out the wind which can penetrate the smallest crack. Whisky barrels served as water tanks for domestic use. Water was pumped from a well in the river. The pump was operated only two hours each day, and if one forgot to fill the house tank it was most unfortunate.

Vacant lots were piled with the refuse that is usually thrown out in daily living. Thanks to the dry air and the hot sun of the desert, there was very little worry over sanitation measures.

There were the usual saloons, stores and restaurants of a mining camp. Dingy rooming-houses had beds that sold for fifty cents a night. There was a drug store, a barber shop, and the inevitable livery stable. Animals came and went, roaming the area; there were always dogs straying about the town, and pigs rooted everywhere.

The town was not treeless. When planted and watered, trees would grow. The soil was rich enough, especially near the river area. As a taken-for-granted location for the cronies of the town to gather and decide the questions of the day (from the national capitol to the silver mines), a low-branched pepper tree stood in front of the Mike Walsh saloon. Here the loafers sat daily and spun their tales of the mines, the road, and their opinions of life in general and the desert in particular. The group was called "The Pepper Tree Club." They enjoyed their place in the sun as they sat hopefully waiting for hand-out drinks which the proprietor often furnished. He realized very little profit from the clubsters, but joined them occasionally, since some of them he had known for a long time. All he asked was that they behaved.

Two hundred men worked in the borax mines and mills. Daggett was a supply point for the borax fields in Death Valley as well as for the Calico borate mines, and its former silver boom. Barstow was only a railroad stop and division point then, and Victorville, about thirty miles toward Cajon Pass, was then mainly a cattle grazing area.

There were no standard work hours for the men employed in the mines and mills and their work-day often ran to ten and twelve hours. The best salaried men were the managers of the borax company, who were paid a hundred and fifty dollars a month, and the next in line who received a hundred and twenty-five dollars a month. White mill workers received two dollars and fifty cents for twelve hours of work; laborers got fifteen cents an hour. Santa Fe railway laborers received ten cents an hour for work on the tracks.

Daggett was never a fancy sort of town. It was just a plain town, geared to bed and feed the men in the mines and mills. There were few women, except the families of some of the workers. Daggett was never a bad town, in the sense that many of the mining camps were so considered.

An evangelist eventually came to Daggett, for it was a town without churches, and he was greatly grieved. What he thought was godlessness was a heavy burden on his soul. Since there was no church building, he held his services in the schoolhouse. The meeting was well attended and the people were generous with their money. When he asked for all who had been saved, to stand, no one stood. After a fervent appeal to his hearers, denouncing the sins of the world, the minister asked those who wanted to be saved, to stand up. Again, no one stood. That was too much for the evangelist. He left town the next day, labeling Daggett as the worst town he had ever known. That was merely one man's opinion — Daggett was never really bad.

When the Santa Fe Railroad came to the region in the 1880s, the Calico silver boom was active. A railway station was constructed with a depot and necessary working sheds. Water was essential, but wells were not easy to bring in. When a well was brought in down in the river bed the water was piped from a steam-engine pump.

Seeking a name for the town that was fast taking hold in the area, Lieutenant-governer John R. Daggett, owner of the Bismarck Mine in the Calico Mountains, was honored by giving it his name. He had constructed the first ore mill for the mines a little toward Yermo, but near the present-day site of Daggett.

Like every other desert mining town of the era, Dagget had its quota of fires. In 1889, everything that could catch fire went up in smoke. Pine lumber had been used in building, with the same dire results as suffered by other towns.

According to records left concerning the early days

of Daggett, the workmen lived under conditions that would seem intolerable today. According to a record left by the late Dix Van Dyke, everyone worked a seven-day week. He said there were four holidays that were always celebrated: St. Patrick's Day, Fourth of July, Thanksgiving and Christmas. According to Van Dyke, St. Patrick's Day took precedence as there were many Irishmen in the town. On that day they all got everything they wanted in the way of food and drink. He wrote: "It was a lucky hobo that got stranded in Daggett on that special day." Everyone wore a green ribbon on his chest, and once "a sacrilegious scamp" tied a green ribbon on a dog's tail and it went down the street waving it. That gesture aroused indignation among the Irish.

One of Daggett's most colorful citizens was Jonas Brown Osborne. He came to California around the Horn in 1852, settling in the San Joaquin Valley to farm. The great general flood of 1862 brought havoc to the San Joaquin Valley as it did to other parts of California. Osborne pulled out and went to Nevada where he accumulated a fortune before returning to California. He spent some time in the Providence Mountains, southeast of Soda Lake, where he operated the famous Bonanza King Mine. It was said of Osborne that he never lost money for anyone, although he was wiped out financially several times. He was very honest in his dealings with others. In 1881 he built the first house constructed in Daggett. It was the finest on the desert at that time. The house was of wooden structure, lined with adobe walls. The building later became a restaurant.

There are few old-timers left in Daggett. One descendant left from a pioneer family is Walter Alf, son of Seymour Alf, who was one of the "Daggett Old Boys." Seymour was an early day teamster who drove a twenty-mule-team, hauling the great wagons of ore. He established a blacksmith shop to service the wagons and teams. His son Walter has restored the old blacksmith shop as it was when his father used it and it is now a museum.

20

Silver Valley

Oh! that the desert were my dwelling place.
Lord Byron,
from *Childe Harold's Pilgrimage*

The Lower Mojave River Valley is not blessed with towns. There have, in past times, been efforts to start settlements, but not many of them matured beyond the few early stage stations or railroad stops. Land development by corporations attempted to colonize certain areas. Sometimes these were carried out in good faith by the developers, even though final results failed to produce either settlements or towns. Other companies used the same methods of development but with less conscientiousness and took all they could from the prospects with little concern about the outcome.

Silver Valley has no distinct boundaries, but stretches out from Daggett in several easterly directions. It takes in the areas out to Newberry Springs (at one time called "Water"), and down to Camp Cady.

Newberry Springs, with its great clumps of alders, willows, and cottonwoods, growing near constantly oozing springs, is a practical experiment in what water will do for a desert. The springs, flowing beneath the black precipices of the Newberry Mountains, have been enclosed with a masonry protection. The springs, since the memory of the white man, have been a stopping-place for travelers from the time of the roaming Indian to the day of the automobile. The site is now a fine resort with the large pool and other recreational features. A modern lake has also been built nearby for enjoyment.

The town of Daggett, born of necessity as a supply town in an era of mining, was not wholly dependent upon the mines or the great wagons that hauled ore from the mines to stamp mills or railroad stations. Wherever a railroad station was placed, a town usually grew, perhaps never to reach anything like ample proportions, but land was always of interest wherever people gathered to work.

Looking out from Daggett there is a great sweeping plain that is pleasing to look upon. The land seemed limitless to newcomers to the desert. Views were resplendent and the colors of the Calico Mountains a few miles away added a sense of grandeur. What a boon all that unused space would be for the land hungry people who were crowded in the dense city areas and wanted land to call their own! Something should be done about that, the land-hungry and the promoters alike felt. Eventually, something was attempted.

In the early 'eighties, Lowery Silver (sometimes called Larry Silva), one of the first discoverers of silver in the Calico Mountains, organized the Silver Valley Land and Water Company. He was made president of the company. The Calico silver mines were still running and borate had been discovered. Times looked pretty good for everyone. After several years of honest efforts to colonize the outlying land near Daggett, the company failed.

The company officials understood mining, but their

knowledge of underground streams and land development was not adequate to resolve the problems that
confronted them. They saw they were failing and when
they sought assistance they were advised to sell the land
to another company, taking irrigation water rights for
payment.

A few years later the Southern California Development Company took over the holdings. This company
did make an honest effort to develop the land, but they
were a little less than honest in their dealings with the
prospects who became interested in their flamboyant
advertising.

A great canal had been built along the river. It was
so constructed that water backed up until it flowed on
the surface of the river. Prospective investors were
brought from Los Angeles by train. Before they were
taken to the river, the canal gate was raised and a large
stream of water flowed into it. It was easy to sell to
prospects after such a sight.

A townsite was laid out and several homes were built
along with a schoolhouse, a post office, and a real estate
building. The town was named Minneola for Minnie
Deterle, wife of the company secretary. Attention was
always called to the black mountain spur, off by Newberry Springs where there was a deposit of iron ore.
The land purchasers were told that the ore would be
brought to the town where a plant would be built to
make Minneola the "Pittsburgh of the West." The buy-
ers moved onto their acreages and tried bravely to raise
crops. They were not used to the soil, nor the climate
they had taken over with the land, and they did not
understand the irrigation system. In five years the project

was abandoned. Because the business reputation of its officers was not of the best, the company could not raise money to carry on, and it went bankrupt. With the failure went the people. For a long time water flowed in the canal, but beds of tules grew in it and trees lined the banks. It lay idle for several years.

About 1902 Theodore Strong Van Dyke and his son, Dixon, a young man of twenty-one, came to the desert for the father's health. The elder Van Dyke was a man of many talents. He had studied irrigation in other areas of the United States, although he had never really farmed. But he became interested in helping in the reclaiming of the desert adjacent to Daggett. During the period when the Southern California Land Company was operating he had looked on in rage at what was being done. He was the one who had suggested that the first development company sell the land for irrigation rights. Now, he was able to convince three of the original company members to go in with him in trying to redeem the land.

The first thing done was to clean out the old canal. The Van Dykes did this by pulling the roots out by hand as they waded through the slush and mud. Year after year the crops they planted would not mature. They were obstinate and would not listen to the advice of the older settlers that it was not worthwhile to spend so much energy on desert land. The vines trailed over the sand, but did not come to fruition. The father's favorite Hubbard squash was a dismal failure. The corn and beans — everything they planted, failed. The winds, blistering and sweeping, were the real cause of the crop failures. Plants were stripped of every leaf. This kept up, but in time the Van Dykes won, in spite of dry years, blighting wind, and the rabbits. Rains came and small floods brought added water.

The efforts of the Van Dykes made an important ranch of their holdings, and they added to the ranch as time and prosperity went on. They had long since left the rented house in Daggett and had their own ranch quarters. The father became the justice of the peace, which office he kept until he died. His son then became the judge and functioned for as long as he lived, dying in 1954. The Van Dykes accumulated about twelve hundred acres which were sold a few years before Dix died. He and his sister kept twenty acres for a home place.

Dix Van Dyke became a desert historian, writing many reams of history for the local newspapers and for historical periodicals. The father and son planted ten thousand trees over their holdings. There was no set plan for the planting. The trees multiplied with the years. Dix was generous with his surplus trees, giving them away to anyone who wanted them for windbreaks and shade. There was a variety of quick-growing trees — cottonwood, Chinese elm, poplars, and the tamerisks and athels which have proved beneficial for quick growing windbreaks.

The story of Silver Valley and the Daggett ranch would not be complete without a word of Mary Beal, desert botanist who came to the Daggett ranch when she was in her early twenties with lung trouble. She had been a librarian in Riverside, California, when she became ill. For two years she lived in a tent house; then a cottage was built for her where she lived out her life and died when in her eighties. Although her health was fully restored she never left the desert she had learned to love and enjoy. She was a self-taught botanist and became an authority on wild flowers and other desert plants. She wrote vividly of her flora. The specimens she gathered can be seen and studied in the University of California in Berkeley. She was much in demand by students of universities and colleges as a guide on field trips over the desert. Such outstanding naturalists as John Burroughs and John Muir asked for her guidance and knowledge when they were making surveys of desert plant life. Mary was practically barricaded by the Van Dyke's ten thousand-plus trees which she had watched multiply and grow tall. She listened to the swish of their music as they brushed across her window panes. Neither Mary Beal nor Dix Van Dyke married. The desert was their great interest.

Dix walked almost every mile of the length of the Mojave River during his lifetime. He was particularly interested in the Old Spanish Trail and the Mojave River.

When the Van Dyke ranch was sold, a resort was built there and called "Tall Trees by the Stream."

Beyond Barstow and Daggett, at the junction of two emigrant trails, the small town of Yermo emerges. The Old Spanish Trail continued on up the Mojave River. The converging trail was known as Old Government Road which crossed the desert between the Colorado River and the Mojave River. The Mojave River creeps through the Yermo region, but is not always noticed, especially today in the high powered cars that speed by. Over it, riding in covered wagons, hauled by horses, mules and oxen, on horseback, and sometimes walking,

A Visiting Day Scene at the Tom Williams Ranch at Otis, now Yermo
Mrs. Williams, at center, was a social leader in the Mojave Desert. Ranch is now
the site of the annual "Calico Days" celebration, reminiscent of "gay 'nineties."

came the emigrants — New Mexicans, 'Forty-niners. Mormons, gold seekers, and adventurers.

Until 1850, Yermo was little more than a spot on the pioneer trail. But it was a welcome sight for the pioneers who were tired from the jolting wagons or from plodding through sand, chilled to the bone from cold and penetrating wind, or ill with the hot winds of California desert summer days.

The Union Pacific Railroad came through Yermo later and assured the town its permanent status. It was near enough to the Calico Mountains that it rubbed elbows with the miners and promoters of the silver mines, and later took the borate boom in its stride. A town cannot live beside such riches and excitement without some of it rubbing off, no matter how small the town. Sixteen years of silver richness; twenty years of borax bonanza, was sufficient to put a town on the map.

When the borax business ceased with Francis Marion Smith closing the mines and going elsewhere, Yermo was well enough on its way to permanence, and the railroads afforded another reason for the town's continued existence. Yermo suffered a couple of bad fires, losing considerable property. Fires are always disastrous, but the old mining towns and supply centers usually snapped right back, rebuilding almost immediately. Yermo was no exception.

Ranches were established along the river, and cattle raising added to the town's worth. Roses bloomed for the gardeners. Tourists poured by as modern transportation advanced with the passing years. Many of these tourists paused to visit the Calico ghost town.

World War II brought a military installation out on the desert a few miles from Yermo — the Holding and Reconsignment Point with its great underground storage facilities. After the war the Point was added to the Marine Corps Depot of Supplies a few miles out of Daggett.

Although the wealth of the Calico mines is no longer apparent from the great gay-colored hills, the beautiful range is there as a backdrop for the drama of desert life. It is rewarding just to be able to gaze on the massive hills with their alluring colors, and to live a little of their past history, or to go into the deep canyons and defiles and see their hidden beauties of nature.

PART VI

Far Reaches of the Mojave

AFTON CANYON CARRIES THE LAST FOUR MILES OF THE MOJAVE RIVER

The waters, always visible here, leave the canyon to enter Crucero Plain where they vanish in the sand, seeking an underground channel to take them to Soda Lake.

21

In Afton Canyon

To see the world in a grain of sand,
And a heaven in a wild flower;
Hold infinity in the palm of your hand,
And eternity in an hour.

William Blake,
from *Auguries of Innocence*

The last few miles of the Mojave River flow through a strange and beautiful canyon that has walls of colored rock structure formed in pipe-organ patterns. The canyon lies in the midst of barren hills and craggy mountains which form a fitting backdrop for the scene of the ancient land. As the waters of the river leave the desert valley lands, seeking an outlet, they pass through a pre-historic dry lake bed which left its geologic story in the alluvial materials that were deposited there. The lake disappeared once, and then in time, reappeared. The waters that filled the lake covered two, and perhaps three, hundred square miles. The waters that accumulated found a weak place in the northeast end of the wall barrier and cut a channel. The lake drained completely. The ancient lake has been given the name of Manix by the geologists because of the railway station that lies in the middle of the old lake area. The gorge that was carved by the long-ago water force was known for many decades as Cave Canyon, but in recent years goes by the name of Afton. The latter name was suggested by the railroad stop of this name at the head of the canyon, and also by a mountain called Afton in the region. It is possible that the former name "Cave Canyon" came from the three caves that were eroded into the canyon walls.

The greenish alluvium of the bed of the old lake (which grew smaller as time went on) may be seen at the entrance to the gorge and a short distance inside the canyon which is covered with a red-bluff conglomerate.[1] In the Manix clays have been found the fossil remains of a mastodon, an antelope, camels, horses and a bird.

The canyon can be entered at either end. Some authorities of the canyon's physical phases advise that it is best to see it by walking a few miles into it from each end rather than trying to drive an automobile completely through. If planning a trip to Afton Canyon it is advisable to consult some reliable authority concerning the details. The seasons of the year make some differences in the entry into the canyon. Strangely, there are not too many who know about the existence of this fascinating canyon which lies only a few miles off the freeway that leads past the Calico Ghost Town area and on to Baker and Las Vegas. The canyon, with its highest walls about four hundred feet above the floor, has been called "Little Grand Canyon."

Ten years ago, having heard and read of the canyon in the far reaches of the desert, I had to see it. So a friend and I made a date with this river of historic significance. We were on our way early, to be able to stop at Calico Ghost Town, which is passed on the way to

---

[1] Jaeger, *California Deserts*, pp. 12-13.

the river's terminus. This was a happy decision as we never saw Calico again in its original ruins — dramatic with its tumbled rock walls that had once sheltered people. We saw the famous Wall Street as it had been left in its last history-making years.

We left the brooding silence of old Calico and reached Proctor's Station in the forenoon. I had been at Proctor's several times when Elmo Proctor, desert pioneer of the far-flung region, was living. He had always been so alive and eager to share his memories of the desert which had been so fulfilling to him and his family. Mr. and Mrs. Proctor had homesteaded in the region. My friend, Betty Estey, and I had arranged for Al, the Proctor's son, to pilot us through the canyon. He had spent his whole life in that area and was familiar with the terrain of the canyon.

Before we left, I had to again handle Elmo Proctor's special desert souvenir, a musical geode. If the geode is tilted just right, it plays the chromatic scale. The Proctors have refused fantastic amounts for that geode and the entire family have vowed they will never break it until it ceases playing the scale. As of September 1969, Elmo Proctor's musical geode is still playing the chromatic scale. He had found the melodious rare geode back in the early 1930s at Cronise Lake.

Mrs. Proctor had packed sandwiches and cake for us all to eat later under a shady tree at Afton Station. Al had a specially-geared army truck for the deep sands of the canyon.

Betty and I had come to see a river. We couldn't wait. So one of us asked, "Where is the river?" And the other echoed the question.

"You are on it!" one of the younger Proctors boasted gleefully.

Knowing something of the river's pecularities, I could well believe it. Though we saw no water at that particular spot, we knew it could be there. We were riding over river waters that had come more than a hundred miles to meet destiny.

We passed the ruins of a house that looked as though it was in the last stages of existence. It had been built in the early homesteading days, we learned, when the corn stood as high as the building. Floods had covered the area, and for several years the soil was rich and productive. The desert willow grows there, and in springtime it throws out its violet scent; its blossoms proudly boast the reputation of being the "orchid of the desert." (The desert willow is not a true willow, but the form of the leaves is similar to the willow; thus its local name.)

Betty and I were so intrigued with the clusters of screw bean from the trees that are plentiful in the canyon that we gathered some to take home with us. Betty made hers into a Christmas wreath. The screw beans are oddly shaped. Clustering, star-shaped pods run from two to ten inches or more in each group and appear as a series of small, dried star-fish, one above the other.

There is an interesting Indian legend about the mesquite. As it is told, there were only three mesquite trees in the world. An Indian was called to the happy hunting grounds by the Great Spirit. He refused to go. After several calls from the Great Spirit, which the Indian still refused to obey, he was asked, "Why do you not want to go?" The Indian replied "There are no mesquite trees in the happy hunting grounds."

The Great Spirit said to the Indian, "Your time has come. You go to the happy hunting grounds and each fall you may come back for a week to eat the fruit of the mesquite tree."

Each fall the Indian came down to earth and sat on top of Dunn Mountain which is in the Cronise area, and watched for the mesquite trees to turn yellow. A wind came one time and broke the yellow branches. The Indian asked the Great Spirit for another week off. The Great Spirit became angry and turned the Indian into a coyote as punishment, and made his mission that of scattering mesquite seed.

Bumping over a no-road wash, Al took his four-wheeler carefully and slowly, and we observed the soil and rocks of the region. Among the things we noted was a wind-blown dam which would help hold waters in leash. Suddenly, we saw water. Assuring ourselves that Mojave's waters were now under us, we spoke of the trickling stream that came slanting toward the wash; its scalloped edges, wiggly, swaying with the small contours of its brook-like bed. That was one of the visible signs of the Mojave River that day. We were as excited as though we had seen a flowing river, confident of its fate.

We looked back and the water was gone. That is the way it sometimes happens — suddenly, when Mojave decides to disappear. It gives one an odd feeling, like the pulling of a curtain quickly over a light. One can see waters go over a spillway and into a reservoir that is there to catch it. But one cannot see through sand.

We had started into the canyon when Al decided we should see the ghost town of Baxter. He turned around in the river and we started on our way, going over a high embankment where there was a rail track. Then the topless army truck balked there on the track. The embankment was almost straight-up-and-down. The left rear wheel skidded and burrowed into the mingled sand and slate gravel. We all piled out of the truck and skidded ourselves to a level stretch of desert. Cautious Al had already braked the truck and had gotten out to survey the situation.

Looking back we could see the great trucks and bulldozers of an iron-mining crew. The heavy equipment sent yellow dust flying, turning the silvery-gray desert holly into tortured shades of dirty pink. That equipment could have taken the truck over the hump in a hurry, but Al had an apparatus that he called a winch, which he used and got the machine over and onto level ground. We all piled back into the truck, ready for more adventure. We were soon at Baxter which is at the mouth of the canyon.

Baxter was once an important rail siding and mining center. Its days of usefulness were about over. It was also soon to lose its name, for there appeared, in another part of the state, another town with the name of Baxter. That caused a lot of confusion. It was as worrisome as two towns of the same name on the same railroad in separate states causing endless trouble with mail. In this case, it often meant heavy equipment going to the wrong locality. The Baxter of the Mojave was changed to Basin.

We came upon a house, the only one in sight. It was in the last stages of existence, about ready to blend into the desert. Sinking floors, rusted bedsprings, a battered hotel cook stove, crude wall cupboards, broken window-panes, empty glass jars turning purple, rusted kettles, the inevitable dented coffee-pot, mateless shoes — all telling a bit of the life gone the way of western mining towns which have no compulsion to live after the ore is gone. There was only the toot of the Union Pacific train, the droning of an airplane, and the swishing winds to give the little old community any life.

Though Afton is walled in by great rock terraces and pinnacles the canyon floor is pastoral. A great meadow spreads out where grasses and tules grow and tree-thickets of athel, willow, cottonwood and mesquite may be found. Until the last decade, the Bighorn sheep picked their way daintily over the crags to come down for water. But the selfish hunters frightened them with guns and it is seldom that one now ventures near the river. Wild horses once roamed the back country, but the same reasons probably hold for their disappearance. Birds are attracted to the river for food, water, and shade.

In the hills and defiles of the back country the rocks are tumbled and creviced. Small canyons lead out to end in stone-rimmed cul-de-sacs. There is plenty in that rugged region to interest the adventurous. Rock-hounds and geologists can find rich fields to hunt bloodstones, jasper, agate, Iceland spar, opalite, carnelians, chalcedony, and onyx. The cliffs are ridged with spires. Pinnacles, tall and slender, are formed in the recesses of the rocks, lifting upward, thousands of them, in evidence of the great surge of water that went through the canyon for millions of years. In some sections the rocks are formed like organ pipes. Had they been hewn by the hands of gifted men they could never have been patterned more perfectly. The gorge is like an outdoor temple.

At one curve in the canyon is a high promontory that is made of colorful rock with pink dominating. The medley of pink, yellow, green, blue, and white makes a spectacular sight. Ledges form stopping-places where ladders were set to enable miners to get to the mines high up on the cliffs. A tramline once brought ore down from magnesium mines. A cable was stretched across the gorge with no support over the canyon's abyss. Great amounts of ore were transported by the "airway" tramway.

There are odd and striking formations in every part of the canyon. Erosion has caused the forming of fantastic shapes, representative of old world ancient fortifications. One section of the area is not unlike a zoo cast in stone.

There is history in that grand little canyon of the wastelands; the history of discovery by a race other than the aborigines. The history of the pathfinders and explorers and their courage in facing a wilderness. There is conjecture and wonder at the Spanish priest who left the foreboding name of "River of Mártires" for the stream he discovered, and did—himself—become a martyr for his pains.

I shall never forget my day in lovely Afton Canyon. Nor will I soon forget the moment I stood beside a small stream of water that was moving, yet it was not going forward—it was sinking down into the sands; but

there was enough flow that a pool rested calmly on top.
I knew. But still I stood in wonderment. The pool
was Mojave's end — one little segment of it. It was a
visible picture of a river's disappearance into the sands
of time — to sink and to spread out infinitely.

Ten years later (in 1967) I again visited the canyon.
It was a summer day this time instead of fall. The sun
was warm and bright, really hot along the freeway as
we left Victorville. The roads had changed with the
progress of time since my first trip to Afton Canyon.
Freeways and interchanges of routes made a great pattern of bridges and loops, and the line of the river
channel was not always in the path of travel.

I wondered if I might find a change down in the
lovely canyon of a decade earlier. I wanted to recap-
ture the feeling of the former visit. I had been in tune,
then, with the river in all its strange features.

We drove first to a bench-land that was high above
the floor of the canyon. We made this side trip to be
able to view the old Indian foot-trail which is still well
defined through the meadowland in the canyon. We
lost the sight of it when it went around a bend in a
clump of trees. The view was beautiful as well as interesting.

Everything below the bench-land was serene and
quiet. Happily we saw water in the river bed, though
the stream was not very wide. We could detect no movement in the water. There were thickets of athel and
tamerisk, carried down, how many years in the past we
will never know, by floods from the desert valley far
upstream. We saw tules and cat-tails too.

The tired old railroad track hugged a wall of the

canyon. The sky was beneficent, and serenity enclosed us; the stillness was unearthly and the silence had depth. We looked across at walls of red and of gray, carved and lined into fabulous patterns by ancient high waters. Later, we would probably he looking *up* at those same tall walls.

The desert bench-land was strewn with an infinite number of small stones, polished to fine lusters by a million years of the elements. We gave our final look at the tan foot-trail, and went down the bench, driving over graveled hills that went up and down, and finally into the Afton entrance.

A few birds flitted in and out of the trees. Now and then there would be a little whirlpool in those seemingly still waters. Birds chirped in the thickets. I did find one spot where water was trickling. Water perhaps had washed out a bit of sand and left a spot looking as though a step had been carved. Water ran over this step into an irregular trough, and to a tiny waterfall of perhaps eight inches. The waterfall met a stone and divided — merrily swirling the waters around it — then met and blended into one tiny stream which seemed to rest on a sandy surface.

I left my little bit of Mojave and joined my friends. Some of them were starting off to search for an old Indian campsite and rumored petroglyphs. The hammer hounds were busy in the countless rocks — of all sizes, shapes, and polish of the elements. Later we met and drove to an intriguing, peaceful spot in the canyon and had our late lunch beneath a high red wall that was patterned in fine-cut ridges. Cat tails grew rank in the nearby water which seemed to stand still. We picked our way over the most firm-looking places in the crusted channel.

We left the canyon the way we had entered, through the two-mile Afton Station area. This entrance adds to the mileage of the canyon's four-mile length. The day had not been long enough for going the full length of Afton Canyon, but we had been joyously reliving history and it was easy to visualize the pioneer padre and his Indian guides trailing through the deep silence between the rock walls. As for myself, I had recaptured the feeling of my former visit to the ancient gorge. I will go back again.

THE SINK OF THE MOJAVE RIVER

Shown here is a part of Soda Lake, usually a dry playa, as it appeared, looking south from Baker, after the river flood of 1938. The lake has appeared thus in other infrequent floods, as in the early months of 1969. The water pouring through the gap washes past the highway and on north to Silver Lake.

Courtesy of San Bernardino County Flood Control District

22

Ancient Lake Mojave

A thousand years hence,
the river will run as it did.

Thomas Fuller,
from *Gnomologia*

When the Mojave River reaches the end of the sculptured canyon, the waters flow out onto Crucero Plain and meander wilfully through the alluvial fan from side to side, groping for channels into which it may find passage for its waters into Soda Lake. After leaving Afton Canyon, the waters have spread over the delta, depositing more sand on the plain.

At the point where the river leaves the confining stream bed in the canyon it loses its carrying power. It becomes a derelict, abandoned on an ocean of sand and gravel, and other detrital material.

There is nothing to see there at the point where the Mojave River leaves the canyon, except an expanse of desert land and the wide, blue canopy of the sky. Crucero is a part of the Soda Lake drainage system of the Mojave River. It is into Soda Lake that the largest amount of the waters of the river goes after it leaves the stream. Silver Lake, into which waters flow when there is a sufficient supply to fill Soda Lake, is also a part of the drainage area.

The Cronise Lakes, on the west side of low hills and

mountains that divide Cronise Valley from Crucero, are
also a part of the drainage system there at the exit of
the Mojave from the canyon. When the Los Angeles
and Salt Lake Railroad was built through Afton Canyon
one of the three caves which were located in the canyon
was shut off.[1] This obstruction caused the Mojave to
lose some of the waters that otherwise would have gone
to Soda Lake, but went, instead, to the Cronise area.
When the Tonopah and Tidewater Railroad, and the Los
Angeles and Salt Lake Railroad crossed in the sand
valley, the junction was called "Crucero," the Spanish
word for "crossing."

Not all the water that the river gathers from its headwater streams reaches the stream's terminus. Much of it
escapes by evaporation. The water that is pumped out
along the river's course for irrigation and domestic use
accounts for a large percentage of the loss. Rampaging
flood waters cause a great waste of the river's flow as it
spreads out on the flat ground and immediately sinks into
the sandy playa. The Mojave's last emergence to the
surface occurs as it enters Afton Canyon and flows to its
outlet at Basin.

Land development was attempted several times in
Cronise Valley. Failure was the outcome in the 1912
efforts and again in the 1930s. The eastern part of
Cronise is the smaller of the two divisions. The waters
in West Cronise are saline and could not be used for
reservoir reserve — one reason for the failure of recla-
mation.

In the winter of 1928-29, work was done on the

---

[1] Jaeger, "The Upside Down River."

Mojave River Sink area which resulted in the discovery of the remains of ancient Pueblo settlements, turquoise mines, and ancient weapons and implements.[2] The investigation of this old Indian culture was sponsored by the San Diego Museum of Man, directed by Malcom J. Rogers, field archaeologist. Pottery and other artifacts which point to the Pueblo culture were found. Dr. Rogers reported:

> What is now the Mojave River sink region once had a permanent Pueblan population. Beside the East Cronise Lake site, several widely separated sites on the south end of the sink produced dominant percentages of Pueblo-type pottery . . On the northwest shore of East Cronise Lake is a site whose Pueblan attributes are sufficiently strong as to identify it as a permanent village of these people.

At the extreme northern end of Soda Lake lies the town of Baker which has outlived its crossroads' history and has become a service oasis, catering to motorists who find themselves between the two dry lakes — Soda and Silver. The Mojave seldom rampages in the Baker area in these later years.

The site of the town of Baker figured historically in the westward trek over the desert. It is sixty miles east and a bit north of Barstow. From Baker are diverging routes to such places of interest as Death Valley and Death Valley Scotty's Castle, Las Vegas, old Lake Mojave, and Calico Ghost Town. Geological records show that the Baker region of the desert was once below sea level. The Mojave, then a forceful stream broke into it and in time the valley floor was raised a thousand feet.

---

[2] Mildred B. Hoover, H. E. and E. G. Rensch, *Historic Spots in California*, revised by W. N. Abeloe (Stanford, 1966), pp. 316-17.

South of Baker, on the surface of nearby Soda Lake, a battle was once fought between the Indians and the United States Army. A Lieutenant Carr, who commanded a small body of soldiers, rode into the mesquite bushes, which were thick and dense, to search for marauding Indians who had been waylaying desert travelers. Several Indians were killed in the fray, others were seriously wounded and were taken as prisoners. The fort established there kept the Indians in subjection and supplied emigrants with water and food.

Soda Lake is some sixty square miles in area and is covered with a white deposit of the chemical content from the water that has flowed from the Mojave River for the countless ages to which the geologists can point. The Mojave River was the one contributor to that ancient lake.

Now and then through recent years floods have been heavy enough to fill Soda Lake and run into Silver Lake. In 1938 Silver Lake held water for several weeks, long enough for regattas to be enjoyed. The floods during the spring months of 1969 reached Silver Lake and remained for several months.

Soda and Silver lakes formed one vast body of water in ancient times. The total area of its drainage system was three thousand five hundred square miles. It was David G. Thompson, government geologist, who suggested that the great ancient lake bed be called "Lake Mohave." He also was the one who applied the name "Little Lake Mohave" to the basin of the Cronise lakes, to the west of the larger basin.[3]

---

[3] U.S. Geological Survey, *Water Supply Papers*, no. 490b (1921), and no. 578 (1929).

The east slope of Soda Lake and a portion of the east slope of Silver Lake are covered with alluvium and the deposits of wind-blown sand. On every windy day the blowing sand builds up against the ridges. This accumulated mass of sand is known as the Devil's Playground. Travel over it is very difficult.

In 1918 there was a small town on the edge of Silver Lake. But in ten years the town was abandoned and only the railway agent and a section crew were left.

Exhaustive studies have been made around the shore line of Silver Lake for Indian campsites. Implements of the stone age are among the artifacts found there. With the weapons, which included the atlatl and spear, the Indians hunted horses, camels, deer, the sloth, and the sabre-toothed cat.

Silver and Soda lakes are connected by a natural trough. R. S. Williamson, who made the survey for railroad routes on the lower Mojave Desert reported the trough as being twenty feet wide and two feet high. It was cut by water in clay soil.

We find our river, the Mojave, has traveled through a course that is approximately one hundred and twenty-seven miles from where it entered the desert floor, below the foothills of the San Bernardino Mountains. As mentioned before, this river follows an ancient channel, and its final outlet in pre-historic times was Death Valley.

What does the average person think when first observing an old dry lake bed? Probably the first conscious thought would be to wonder what happened to the water. What did happen to make those fresh water lakes dry up? What happened to make the pasture lands and lush banks disappear? Why did the desert happen? Why did time seem to stand still?

The answer is simple — it stopped raining.

Now there is only a great waste of flat and lonely land down there where once a mighty river flowed through its valley and canyons, bringing immense amounts of sand into a vast body of fresh water abounding with fish. What a joyous country it must have been before aridity took the place of pluvial waters.

It seems so limitless with only sand and sun and salt-bushes, though it has a stark and hungry beauty. Anything as ancient as that great expanse of desert, which has had time rolling over its emptiness for so long, is bound to gain a sort of dignity — the dignity of simplicity.

So simple — the sunlight shimmering on the space, sand, gravel and salt-encrusted nodules, over which winds blow and carry the infinite grains of sand, so fine and powdery, to form the dunes and ridges.

This is the Sink of the Mojave.

Index